Hall Group Unlimited LLC Presents

The Diamond Project

A Different Education Inspired by Acres of Diamonds Written by: Russell Conwell

By: Eric D. Hall

Education- The development and training of one's *mind, character, skills,* etc., as by instruction, study or example.

(Latin Origin) Root Word Educo- which means to pull out or to draw from within.

"Education is the ability to take on life's situations"
John G. Hibben

What Is a _Diamond?_- *said the old priest, "A diamond is a congealed drop of sunlight." Now that is literally scientifically true, that a diamond is an actual deposit of carbon from the sun.*

WORK DILIGENTLY ON EACH DIAMOND AND YOU AND THOSE CONNECTED TO YOU WILL OWN THE FUTURE

Contents

Fresh Strat	6
The Story	12
F-Diamond	16
L-Diamond	44
The most powerful of all emotions	45
P-Diamond	77
D-diamond	91
S-Diamond	104
LET'S START DIGGING	131
The Diamonds In Others	138

Chapter I

Fresh Start

Clearing Technique Before Starting the Diamond Project Ho'oponopono- It's of Hawaiin Origin

- ❖ *I Love You*
- ❖ *I'm Sorry*
- ❖ *Please Forgive Me*
- ❖ *Thank You*

As simple and basic as these four statements are they are also profound and can be the catalyst to a better life. Many people are hindered from moving forward because they lack, or never been exposed to authentic and genuine Love. Maybe because of how they were raised along with other circumstances and now as an adult they may struggle with showing it, making it hard to receive it. The same is true for the principle of forgiving and asking for forgiveness. When you don't forgive it becomes toxic to your inner-most self and corrupts your judgment when it comes to people and new relationships, while never apologizing or asking for forgiveness diminishes your quality of life and impedes per- sonal growth. Every moment where necessary, show gratitude and appreciation because it opens doors for more! Life will always give you back what you put out. Some say *"You Reap What You Sow"*, others call it *"Carma"*, my favorite is *"Seed Time- Harvest Time"*. While they mean the same thing *"Seed Time- Harvest Time"* reso- nate the most with me because of the word *TIME*. The word time suggests that at some point you will get a return from the seeds you plant. While there are many dimensions to this statement I will mention a few. First of all, many of us live as though we have an unlimited amount of time here on planet earth so we spend our time expecting a harvest first instead of planting accordingly. We want Love, Gratitude and Appreciation from others but we offer a scarce amount, instead being ungrateful and bitter. It's like putting a rock in the soil/dirt and expecting to see a rose in six months. The other point to remember is the way to get anything in life is to first give it away. I can recall many times when I needed encourage- ment and the best remedy was encouraging someone else. I prom- ise, it works! It almost seems abnormal in today's society to give first but it is without a doubt the surest way to receive. Like the lost art of volunteering that many folks will not do if it's not a mandate from court or to pay off a debt. Try to volunteer with no guarantee of any reward, compensation or benefit and watch the opportunities that appear in your life, but this act must be authentic and with the right intentions.

Galatians 6:9

"The one who sows to please his sinful nature, will reap destruc- tion; the one who sows to please the spirit, from the spirit will reap eternal life. Let us not become weary in doing good, for at the proper time we will reap a harvest if we do not give up. Therefore as we have opportunity, let us do good to all people, especially to those who belong to the family of believers."

DON'T TAKE IT PERSONAL

This point will be reiterated throughout this project because it can work against you if it's not understood. When you make a decision to make a fresh start in any area of your life there will be people
in your life that will not understand, believe or support your efforts. I am not talking about strangers or folks that you just met. I'm talking about relatives, good friends, spouses, long time work colleagues and other trusted individuals. Your first point of clar- ity should be an understanding that your purpose and vision was not giving to them, therefore they will never see it like you see
it. The second point of clarity is your need for strength and focus because solitude and loneliness will be the dominant presence most times. The third point of clarity is that help, sup- port and some- times resources will show up through strangers and those you meet along the journey that may be on a similar journey, or they simply believe in what you're doing. It's not personal even though many times it feels and looks personal especially if someone that you were extremely helpful to does not reciprocate the help or support. Forgiving is one of the hardest of the human abilities but until we get a firm under- standing of its danger in our lives we will take things personal and miss opportunities. I trust that this project will give you additional tools to broaden your perspective and thrust you into your destiny allowing you to move past disappointment and resentment.

IT'S NEVER TOO LATE

"Procrastination is the thief of Time" **Edward Young**

Many of us live as though we have an unlimited supply of time therefore feel like we can get to the important stuff later. Every minute that we waist is a minute that can never be re-cooped. You can always get back money that you spend or a car that you lose but time moves in one direction, forward. Although it is never too late for a fresh start we must reflect on whatever time we took for granted and be sure not to let that happen during this new part of our journey. Make every minute count and always ensure success through fulfilling endeavors and more productive activities. Get out of the habit of just passing the time as many of us do. This does not mean that we ignore rest and relaxation, fun in the sun or good ole down time but only as a reward for hard work and to rejuvenate the spirit and energy to go back into battle and achieve greatness.

THE POWER OF FORGIVENESS

What Do You Say

Several years back I was co-producing a show as well as perform- ing in it. The show was called "From Gospel to Hip-Hop and all in Between". It was a music lineage performance that celebrated the historical timeline of black music. I was working on the show with a great friend, Mr. Haywood Fennell on the entire production. The total team was made up of about 20-30 people including segment producers and performers. I produced the hip-hop segment, which closed out the show. Little did I know that while doing the Lord's work that my life would change forever. During one of the produc- tion rehearsals I had the pleasure of conversing with a phenomenal woman. She was the mother and leader of the female gospel group that performed in the show. She was complimenting me on how respectful I was and about the show. The more we talked the more we began to make a connection to the people we knew. She then asked the last name of my family, which brought on another element of a life-changing conversation. I told her the name and the neighborhood. She made an instant connection to the neighbor- hood but not the name. After a while it clicked and she said "OH MY GOD" your related to the (   ) and said my families last name. The next question was who is your mother? I answered and her mouth dropped to the floor. I asked her what was wrong and she said . I was totally lost for words and could not imagine her feelings at that moment. When I was five years old my mother was in a fight and the other woman had a knife, so someone watching the fight gave my mother a knife to make it a fair fight. My moth- er ended up killing the woman in self-defense and was sentenced to 5-7 years in prison. For the next seven years I had no physical mother. That alone is another book. *("Thank God For Grandpar- ents")* As the story goes the woman hugged me and I hugged her back. She began to cry and so did I. After about ten minutes she looked at me and said *"I finally forgive your mother and your family because I have met you, and you are a great young man, Thank God for you"*. At that moment I was given back seven years of my lost childhood with my mother. It made me realize the importance of character and a good name. God hides everything

in a moment. At that moment 25 plus years of resentment, anger and who knows what else was released from this woman of God towards my family. I once heard that carrying around anger and resentment towards anyone was like drinking poison and hoping that the other person would die from the poison. There were so many things that I learned from this seemingly sad moment. It was actually a wonderful moment. Not only the power of forgiveness, but also when you are working in your purpose lives will change. Become a person of change through excellence and hard work.

Because my mother has gone on to be with Lord this project is dedicated to her. She never got to mine for the Diamonds that God placed in her due to life's circumstances and her personal choices. The world never got to experience The Good, The Bad and The Beautiful person named Diane Hall. Full of Love and Life with amazing intelligence is who she was. Through my work you will know her and that is why this project is dedicated to her. She gave me life and that enough to always Love and remember our connec- tion. Thank You mommy, I Love You!

The Story

Acres of Diamonds: by Russell H. Conwell (1843-1925)

Part 1: Russell H. Conwell's Inspiration

Russell H. Conwell was inspired by underserved young people with a desire to go to college after they graduated High School. The only problem was that they could not afford to go to college due to financial constraints. With a burning de- sire to help them, plus passion for the next gen- eration, he did over 6,000 speeches and raised millions of dollars, which became seed money to start Temple University. Amazingly he con- ducted 1 speech titled: Acres of Diamonds. Mr. Conwell's body of work goes way beyond this achievement and will be worth your time to ex- plore the journey of this Great Diamond Min- er. With his expansive resume you will realize that his primary duty was to mine the diamonds within every person who crossed his path and then show them how to do it for themselves.

Part 2: Russell Conwell's (Acres of Diamond's)

This is a story of a man who owned a significant piece of property. It was during a time that folks were coming from around the world to find dia- monds, all because a few people on the African Con- tinent discovered diamond mines. Looking to get in on the action, the gentlemen sold his prop- erty for little to nothing in pursuit of diamonds and riches. The person who acquired the property discovered a blue stone in his creek in the back of the property and displayed it on his mantle. One day he had a visitor who was intrigued by the beau- ty of the stone. When he asked of its find- ings, the visitor was shocked to hear the land owner say that he had those stones sprinkled throughout his creek in the back. It turned out to be the most productive diamond mine on the entire African Continent. The man who sold the land never dis- covered what he already possessed. He ended up committing suicide once despair and failure over- whelmed him. The point of this story is self-ex- plan- atory. The man never took the time to survey his own land. What if he cultivated and dug up parts of his land. Maybe if he examined the creek and tested the soil, hired help to cover more ground he would've discovered the riches right beneath his feet. This is the story of 90% or more of the popu- lation. Even without the suicide most people will live and die without ever discovering the Acres of Diamonds within themselves. Ideas, thoughts and cre- ative ability that are choked out because life happens and we expect someone else to have the an- swers and the solutions that we already possess.

Part 3: My Inspiration/ Intelligent Objectivity

This story was my life for many years. I was search- ing and searching for answers in all the wrong places. After years of pain and adversity I began my journey towards personal development and getting better. As the new information began to broaden my perspective and re-shape my view it also enhanced my personal philosophy. How I saw the world and my-self in it was changing. For many years I believed that success was only for a cer- tain type of individual, from a chosen ethnic group, financial status or political party. My reality and achievements were stifled by these limiting beliefs. The books I began to read gave me exposure to the possibilities and allowed me to accomplish new goals, build confidence and change the course of my life. I realized that successful people had the same challenges and adversities as I did and many times, much worse.
In my journey I had an aha mo- ment and realized that success was a choice. Hap- piness was a choice. Prosperity was a choice. Great relationships were a choice. It did not matter what life circumstances I faced. Now as a husband, Father and community advocate my daily work is rooted in helping individuals discover what they already possess. The first challenge is removing obstacles that we all face. The second challenge is altering the internal conversation that we have with ourselves about ourselves. Is this conver- sation rooted in doubt, fear and worry, and if so, let's change it. If not, we never get to creativity, inventions, ideas and the life we truly desire all because we search for answers everywhere but in ourselves. The Diamond Project will broaden your perspective and awareness about your internal gifts. It will also become a living source of on-go- ing support, while acting as the gift that keeps on giving. It can be the tool in your toolchest that can be used at every level of personal and financial achievement. You are here to leave your mark on the world. You have no choice; the next generation depends on it! Re- member; whatever you don't fix, those who follow will inherit it.

Part 4: The Creator's Inspiration

Raw Materials that he placed in the earth(Trees, Gold, Steel, Air, Water, Oil, food). When God creat- ed the earth and gave humans dominion over it, he made sure that every desire of our hearts could manifest in the earth by putting all of the raw materials in the earth.

Simultaneously placed in us was something called Potential? The raw material called potential had two partners called Heart and Mind. With these three raw materials placed in us we can all live a life full of advancement, growth and productivity. This is God's intention for us in the earth. The limits and lack of accomplish- ments comes from us. The goals we never achieve is not because we started with a deficit. If you only take one thing from this entire project, began to view yourself as an asset and not a liability, a priceless Diamond and nothing less.

Foundation
Family
Faith
Finance
Fitness

Chapter II
F-Diamond

Faith- Confidence or trust in a person or a thing. Belief that's not based on proof. A system of religious beliefs.

Family- A basic social unit consisting of parents and their children, considered as a group, whether dwelling together or not. Any group of persons closely related by blood as parents, children, aunts, uncles and cousins.

Fitness- Health! Capability of the body of distributing oxygen to muscle tissue during increased physical effort. The ability of a popu- lation to maintain or increase its numbers in succeeding generations. The genetic contribution of an individual to the next generations gene pool relative to the average of the population, usually measured by the number of offspring or close kin that survive to reproductive age.

Finances- The monetary resources, as of a government, company, organization or individual; revenue

Foundation- The basis or groundwork of anything. The natural or prepared ground or base on which some structure rests.

Faith

Matthew 18:19

"If two of you agree on earth concerning anything that they ask, it will be done for them by my Father in Heaven"

Quote "Faith is the oil that will remove the friction from life"

On New Year's Day (22nd Anniversary), while digesting a deli- cious meal prepared by my beautiful wife, she made a discovery that I had to steal. My 15 year old son had this conversation on his facebook page. Sometimes while raising teenagers, parents feel as though they have lost a grip on them, especially with commu- nication. We are blessed to know that his view of God is about a personal relationship and God in his heart and not about religion that can sometimes compromise the relationship.

A Conversation worth reading:

Professor: Did God create everything?

Student: Yes

Professor: If so, then God also created evil. Therefore, God is evil.
(student stood up and asked) Do dark exist Sir?

Professor: Yes! It does.

Student: Dark doesn't exist. Dark is only the absence of light. Just like evil, it is only the absence of God in human's hearts.

Faith is something you can't see with the natural eye. Faith applies to every area of your life and this is true whether or not you have a specific religion that you believe in or not. No matter where your faith is you can grow in your faith, in fact life will make sure of it. The other component to faith is activating your plan to live the highest quality life possible with unequivocal faith. When action is present you will encounter many coincidences that will propel you closer to your dreams and goals. Les Brown defines a *coincidence* as God's way of remaining anonymous. Others should never have control over your faith. You may ask, how is this possible? If you observe many people in their faith walk the level of faith they have is filtered through others. Those others can be their pastor, elders or those they assume are more spiritually mature than they are. The downside to this type of faith is, if any of the individuals you've deemed more spiritual than you fall from grace or suffer a public embarrassment from whatever, your faith can be destroyed. Build your faith on a personal connec- tion and relationship with God.

Romans 8:38-39

"For I am persuaded beyond doubt (am sure) that neither death nor life, nor angels nor principalities, nor things impending and threatening nor things to come, nor powers. Nor height nor depth, or anything in all creation will be able to separate us from the Love of God which is in Christ Jesus our Lord."

Psalm 37:19

"In the days of famine they will have abundance"

Don't fear the person that can kill the body, fear the person that

can kill the spirit and the soul." Bishop T. D. Jakes

Genesis 28:15

"I will not leave you until I have done what I have promised"

Psalms 34:10

"Those who seek the LORD shall not lack any good thing"

Fitness

Excerpt from *CHARACTER* by Samuel Smiles (1812)

"It requires strength and courage to swim against the stream, while any dead fish can float with it."

Life is a workout and it could care less about your race, size, gender, socio-economic status or how much money you got in the bank. You will go through rigorous, physical and many times life threatening challenges similar to working out if you live long enough. Life will build your strength, confidence, focus and emo- tions like working out builds your muscles. Your muscles are built and conditioned from pushing against the resistance; much like how life's resistance and obstacle's that will confront you. As you conquer and victoriously make it through all that life will bring you, this will activate your faith and either strengthen it or weaken it. The same is true when working out because you can strength- en and build muscles, or you can strain and damage muscles. So today, I welcome you to the gym of life.

Every person has 600 muscles and only uses about 400 for ev- ery- day use and application. We underutilize muscles like we do our brainpower and our potential to achieve greatness. From this point forward decide to tap into all of your God-Given potential. You must be intentional in this effort, merely think- ing about improving your health and physical ability will not happen by osmosis.

Remember that a broken body has a lot less limitations than a broken spirit!

Isaiah 40;29-31

"He gives strength to the weary and increases the power of the weak. Even youths grow tired and weary, and young men stumble and fall; but those that hope in the Lord will renew

their strength. They will soar on wings like eagles; they will run and not grow weary, they will walk and not be faint".

We must take care of our bodies because it is the only place we have to live. No matter where you move to, whether city, state or country your body will be with you. Many people take care of their homes, cars and pets better than their own vessel. Some people with a green thumb take care of and water their plants everyday but drink things that are more harmful to the body than good.

"Fatigue makes cowards of us all" Vince Lombardi

Words of Wisdom from Eric D. Hall Jr., 15 years old at the time: *"When you're in shape you feel good about yourself, which rais- es your confidence and allows you to take risks. When you take risks you succeed."*

Most people see taking care of their bodies and working out as tedious and boring and many times it's a task for folks. One of the reasons is because it's always a short term commitment connected to an event or time of year. You'll hear people say "I have to lose weight for my sister's wedding" or, "I want my body to be tight for the summer". If you see working out as a way of life and connect it too something more valuable and long term you may develop the discipline. Here are a few of the many statements you can make to yourself and others. "I need to be healthy to enjoy my children." or "I need to break the cycle of high blood pressure in my family by adjusting my diet and regular physical activity". These are more lifestyle changes as opposed to a task for a short term goal.

My wife and I just finished our 10-day green smoothie cleanse and the results were amazing even-though this was our first time. In my initial research I found that the goals of this cleanse was to clean toxins from your body and detox- ify your system. Although I did not know exactly what that meant I saw belly fat go down that hadn't gone done even after many sets of crunches and other exer- cise. While this was totally new to me it was utilized by thousands around the world. As your journey to a healthier you takes off just know that the how to information does exist and you are not alone even-though there will be times of solitude.

Food for thought:

Make a mental shift as it relates to your health. If a doctor ever says "what you have is incurable". Interpret it to mean that you are curable from with-In.

Inertia - Objects at rest tend to stay at rest until acted upon by an outside force. Objects in motion tend to stay in motion until stopped by an object not in motion.

Connect this to your personal life and you can draw a parallel to people and circumstances in your life that either slow you down or assist you in moving forward. Most times we know who they are but because they are friends, family or close colleagues we will allow their influence to take us off track. The same is true for those who edify and propel us towards our dreams and goals.

E-Motion- is Energy in motion

"One of the most potent forms of energy is thought" Bob Proctor

Potential is also like energy, unlimited, no beginning and no ending.

Is it possible to maximize our energy to be more Effective, Cre- ative, Productive and Happy (JOYFUL)?

What do you know about Mental Tension and Structural Ten- sion and their connection? One point I will share is that tension always wants to relieve itself. While there are many I will share 3 points relating to mental tension:

Point 1: Anger is a form of emotional tension that starts as mental tension because we thought first and then felt the anger. Did you know that when you are angry your body will build up toxins that are harmful to your health? Anger turns into stress, stress then magnify ailments in the body that may be minimal. Most of us never connect our physical health to negative emotions like anger, bitterness, envy and hate. When these emotions are present towards someone it's like drinking poison and wanting them to die. Yes, that is how harmful those emotions are to your physical well being. This does not mean that these emotions make you or me bad indi- viduals because they are a part of our human nature. We can also use these emotions to fuel positive change in our lives to impact others instead of letting them control our decisions in a bad way and erode our health.

Point 2: Visual Consumption is a form of mental tension. Did you know that the average person watches 4-6 hours of television per day. Negative news gets a great deal of our attention and de- creases our personal power. Watching violent programming de- creases the strength of the immune system, while watching comedy and uplifting programming builds up your immune system. When your mental capacity is over loaded there is mental tension because the creative, imaginative and goal oriented aspects of your mind is constantly at war with your visual consumption.

Point 3: Outward Manifestation is what we see and what others see as a result of our feelings and thoughts. Our life, how we live, what we say, how we respond to problems, how we treat ourselves and others. Let's connect the first two points to outward manifesta- tion. Structural tension is the analogy I will use. Imagine a brick on top of a bed of ice that is thick enough to hold its weight but when the ice is no longer thick enough, what happens, the ice breaks.
What about a house that is supported by wood beams that over time began to erode from termite damage. A few months ago here in Massachusetts many people lost their homes because the homes were beachfront and they were built on foundations

that were part- ly supported by sand. A Tropical storm with excessive rain and ex- tremely high tides washed away key parts of the foundation which no longer supported the rest of the structure, resulting in structural tension and eventually homes lost. Now can you see the parallel to our lives? If tension has to relieve itself no matter what the cir- cumstances are that means there will be an outward manifestation, good or bad. Earlier I spoke about mental and emotional tension like anger, which we all know can lead to violence or abuse. Anger unresolved can make a person turn to alcohol and drug abuse, be- coming unfaithful to loved ones and more. This is just the tip of the iceberg when it comes to the many manifestations of mental and emotional tension. Also anger is only one emotion of many. I spoke about visual consumption as a form of mental tension because we never connect how we feel and think to what we watch. As you take back control of your life in every area remember that your physical body is one leg on a three leg stool and the other two legs are your mental(mind) capacity and your emotional(heart) capaci- ty. If there is excessive tension on either of the three the other two are vulnerable. We will all experience mental, emotional and phys- ical tension, the key is to find healthy, productive ways to relieve it. Once you're aware you must solve it, talk about it, get help, get rid of it or whatever it takes to reduce harmful and destructive results.

Family

Acronym

*F*ocus *A*nything *M*ajor *I*n *L*oving *Y*ourself

Family is your first and most important Mastermind Group as defined by Napolean Hill.

Family is where you get your first lessons on the power of good
relationships or the detriment of bad relationships.

These relationships take care, nurture and a little imagination. They also take time and effort to strengthen them.

All relationships like flowers, once they bloom, still need water,
sun and other care.

"Don't let the enemy have your family. Fight with every breath you got" Creflo Dollar

Zig Zigler famously said "If you have a Home-Court advan- tage you can win everywhere else". Which means every relation- ship in your home should be solid. This will build and boost your confidence when you face outside challenges. I just celebrated
my 22nd Year Anniversary and since the day I said I do, my wife and I agreed that we would always have Peace and Love in our house because negativity, frustration and turmoil was right outside waiting to come in. Peace and Love became our armor in building a quality life for our family even through storms. We have also witnessed countless marriages and families who are torn apart simply because outside influences infiltrated the home. Having a big heart can sometimes work against you. Take for instance the person who takes in a family member because they have nowhere else to go, but this is the family member that brings crisis and trouble into your home. It is your goal to help them, only to realize that their goal is to

use you as a crutch for the moment. They have no intentions of changing and your spouse is aware of this. Now, arguments become the norm because you can't turn your back on a family member. Your children are influenced by the negative habits of the family member you took in. Can you see the chain reaction when you allow the home environment that you worked so hard to create is uprooted because your big heart worked against you? I am not suggesting that you turn your back on a family member or a friend in need but be aware of any patterns that can change your home's culture. There are many ways that you can help if they want it. You must build all significant relationships with this same caution and care. Below are some key relationships that you may have.

Fact: *86% of marriages end for non-severe reasons*

Significant Relationships

- Yourself
- Spouse
- Family members
- Your children
- Co-workers
- Colleagues
- Church members
- Business partners
- Community stakeholders

Lets identify the Quality of the relationships that apply to you and measure them by the four areas listed

- Time (Quality & Quantity)
- Consistency

- <u>Deposit or Withdrawal</u>
- <u>Increase or Decrease</u>

Time with friends and family should always be memorable. When I first had children I believed that quality time was enough and that quantity didn't matter that much. So if I spent ten minutes with my children and it was a great ten minutes then I did my part in the time commitment department. This was my logic until I really began to understand the value of time and that it was not an un- limited commodity. The best thing I could have done is realize the importance of quantity-time along with quality-time. So planning family time should be intentional and purposeful and not the typi- cal, we'll find time eventually. This should be your attitude with all significant relationships in your life. Every-day that passes you can no longer have back. Here is a note to folks striving to accomplish great things in their life. Although ac- complishing goals will cause us to make some time sacrifices and relationships suffer in the process, we must make sacrific- es that we can live with. For exam- ple if this weekend is an important business meeting but it's also your child's 8th grade graduation, what do you do? I am going to my child's gradu- ation because there will never be another 8th grade graduation for my child. My child may be affected for years be- cause of my absence. There are individuals who would sacrifice the graduation and justify their absence in the name of building for the future. I am no stranger to making sacrifices and part of this point is about perspective also, just remember the ultimate question ***"can you live with the sacrifice, especially when the lost time can never be re-cooped"?*** Once you truthfully answer that question proceed accordingly, you are not right or wrong. My primary reason for becoming an entrepreneur was for flexibility of time and the ability to enjoy the precious mo- ments that so many people miss because of work or business obligations. My 16 year old son can truthfully say that I never missed a field trip in elementary and my 9 year old daughter says proudly that my daddy only missed one field trip but mommy was there. That matters to me but it may not matter to someone else.

Decide to focus a small part of your life's mission on being a deposit in people's lives, especially your family. Also give them a sense of increase because of your presence and influence. A simple way of measuring this is by asking these four questions.

Do family and friends think more of themselves and take action because of me? *(Deposit)*

Do family and friends believe in themselves and as a result reach for new goals because of me? *(Increase)*

Are co-workers disappointed when I'm not present because I pro- duce and unify the team? *(Increase)*

Does my presence shift a negative mood in different environments?

(Deposit)

This applies to all other key relationships in your life that are listed above. Take note of how you are impacted by these same connec- tions to the people in your life. By no means do I advise you to allow family or friends do the opposite to you. Withdraw instead of deposit, decrease instead of increase. Are you familiar with what withdrawal or decrease looks like? Be aware of these subtle state- ments that can be disguised as concern. An older gentlemen said something to me many years ago and it made no sense at the time, although life experiences have supported his statement, he said **"Good intentions paved the road to hell".** Here are a few state- ments to look out for that can easily appear to be good intentions: This is in the context of you embarking on a new venture, starting a business, going back to school or inventing something.

- YOU DON'T HAVE A DEGREE
- YOU DON'T HAVE THE MONEY
- YOU'RE NOT CONNECTED ENOUGH
- THAT'S IMPOSSIBLE
- NOBODY IN YOUR FAMILY EVER DID THAT
- HAVE FUN AND WORRY ABOUT THAT LATER
- YOUR YOUNG YOU HAVE PLENTY OF TIME
- YOU CANT DO THAT BECAUSE YOU HAVE KIDS
- YOUR NOT THE RIGHT RACE
- I DID THAT AND IT DIDN'T WORK FOR ME
- WHAT IF YOU FAIL
- IT'S TOO RISKY

These are key indicators that must not go uncheck, unless medioc- rity is your ultimate goal. If that's the case then this entire project may be of little use to you, on the other hand you would not have gotten this far if you weren't on the journey towards greatness. The following quote applies to many people in our society. Take the following statement and remove it from a physical condition and apply it to other areas of our human existence like mental, emo- tional and relational.

"I freed a thousand slaves. I could've freed a thousand more if only they knew they were slaves" Harriet Tubman

In closing this section on family I would like to bless you with a piece of writing by my son Eric D. Hall Jr. I guess this is his intro- duction to the publishing world. This is a heart-felt piece and I was honored to be his father. Thank You Son!

The Starting Five

What do you call the clique of people that are closest to you? That you know will always be there for you no matter what. I call mine the Starting five also known as my family. In basketball every team has a starting five. The starting five, start the game off. They're preferably the best five players on any team. Their job is to get the team off to a good start in the game. I'm a part of a starting five off the court. This line up consist of my mother, father, brother, sister and I. We are the starting five. They are the most important people to me and they have been there all my life. Well my sister joined the team back in 2005' so she's sort of new.

First we have to the floor is my mother. Lisa Hall. She is the back bone of the team. She is the heart and soul. Her personality is the very stern but most loving kind of personality you will ever find. A hard working woman that will literally do just about anything for her family even if that means walking on her hands to China from Roxbury. There's nothing that would stop her from providing for. She works for hours and still comes home and would try to cook for us or do laundry. My father does not allow that..!

That brings me to my father. Eric Sr. The protector, pro- vider, comedian, role model. He goes out of his way to make sure we are safe at all times. My father is the reason why I am who I am today. I use him as a mirror, I try to copy all of his ways. He really knows how to make a crowd of people laugh. Being a bore is almost impossible for him. There is never a time that goes by when I'm around him and I don't laugh. I feel like that is where I get my humor from. The way he carries himself is how I want my children to view me. When I have children I will without a doubt copy his skills. And let's not forget he is co-chef in the house. He and my mother are the best tag team chefs you will ever meet.

Next we have my older brother Jahlin Hall. Now this guy has literally helped and guided me through just about everything. If there is anything I need he is there to help my sister and I. Some say we can pass as twins, not only because we have almost the same personality but we also look the same. All I need is a beard and some extra time in the sun. We play the exact same sports. I can probably go to his school and be him for a day. There is noth- ing he does not know about me. I remember one time when we were playing basketball and literally no one on the court was able to beat us not even the adults. I find it funny how one day we are arguing over action figures to next debating over which college he should attend next year. With my brother and I age means nothing. He is 20 years old and I'm only 16. I don't know if it's because I'm mature or if it's because he is still a big kid at heart.

The newest member of the team is my 9 year old sister Na- lani. She is definitely the most mature little girl I have ever known.

I want to see what her brain looks like because there is no way it is normal. Her IQ is probably higher than some of my friends today. Once you get past her sass, she is extremely loving and
very caring and would hurt someone for one of us. She is the little girl version of my father with a hint of my mother in the mix. For someone who is that small she will be heard and seen just because of the kind of person she is. My sister is a "fashion designer danc- er". That is her career right now. Her passionate character will get her to very great places in the future. I feel bad for the person that tries to tell her no in the future because when she sets her mind to something she will make sure she will get it even if it means being patient for a really long time. She sometimes tries to strong-arm my brother and I despite the fact that we are so much bigger than her. Nalani who is the toughest 9 year old ever.

These four people that I just mentioned are not just family members but they are my teammates. We play this game called life, but this game is not to played without a team and my team is Team HALL. Without my team to assist me I don't know where I would be right now. This team's starting 5 is the best starting five you will ever find..!.

Finance

Golden Nugget: **Financial Success without fulfillment is not beneficial.**

Proverbs 23:4/5

"Do not wear yourself out to get rich; have the wisdom to show restraint. Cast but a glance at riches, and they are gone, for they will sprout wings and fly off to the sky."

Mis-Conception: If I had more money my life would be better. We somehow think that our financial situation is a math prob- lem, but it's actually a mind problem.

Joshua 1:8

"You will make your way prosperous, and then you will have good success."

Before I go further into this section on finance I would like to set the proper context for this subject. Transition your mind from thinking about money and think prosperity and abundance. There are critics that are against what has been labeled "prosperity min- istry", which in most cases it's simply because of a misinterpreta- tion of the definition of prosperity. Critics only speak against the prosperity message because their perspective is limited to believe that it promotes the possession of material items. While material blessings are a part of prosperity and abundance it's only a frac- tion in comparison to the totality of what God wants for your life. **Prosper (Greek** *euodoo***) – "***To help on one's way, act wisely, and be successful and wealthy"* it stems from receiving God's wisdom and obeying his instructions on your journey. As you continue this section on finances and gain tools and how- to information, keep in mind that total prosperity includes good health, strong marriag- es, quality relationships and spiritual enlightenment and most all helping others.

3rd John 1:2

"Beloved, I pray that you may prosper in all things and be in health, just as your soul prospers.

It is Okay to be Wealthy!

Many people quote a phrase from the bible that is incorrect, "mon- ey is the root of all evil", when it clearly says that "the love of money is the root of all evil". Money is not meant to control you or become something you praise. Your spiritual and moral integ- rity should never be compromised because of money. Family and community should never be second to monetary gain. If you are fortunate through your good works, creations or ideas to accumu- late wealth it is your duty to become a blessing to others. Whatever it takes you must begin a process to develop a healthy perspective about money. Many of my limiting beliefs came from the lack of money, resources and information. Today, do a money self-assess- ment. Make sure you develop a healthy understanding of money and not to demonize what we need. We the people give it its value and make it good or bad.

2nd Corinthians 9:6-9

"Remember this: Whoever sows sparingly will also reap sparingly, and whoever sows generously will also reap gener- ously. Each man should give what he has decided in his heart to give, not reluc- tantly or under compulsion, for God Loves a cheerful giver. And God is able to make all grace abound to you, so that all things at all times, having all that you need, you will abound in every good work. As it is written:

Time tested wisdom of Ben Franklin from his book titled: "The Way to Wealth"

"Diligence is the mother of good luck, and God gives all things to industry. Then plough deep, while sluggards sleep, and you shall have corn to sell and keep. Work while it is

called today, for you know not how much you may be hindered tomorrow. Never leave that to tomorrow what you can do today." Ben Franklin

Questions to Ponder

1. What if you could earn in 1 day what your par-ents earn in a whole month?
2. What if you earn in 1 month what you use to earn in 1 year?
3. What disciplined activity would it take for question 1 and 2 to become a reality or is that too big for you to fathom?

"You can't manage time, you can only manage activity". Earl Nightingale

Let's Explore The Possibilities

Deuteronomy 15;4-6

"However there should be no poor among you, for in the land the Lord your God is giving you to possess as your inheritance, he will richly bless you, if only you fully obey the Lord your God and are careful to follow all these commands I am giving you today. For the Lord your God will bless you as he has promised, and you will lend too many Nations but will borrow from none. You will rule over many Nations but none will rule over you."

When you can't provide for your family it affects you and your ability to have peace. Things that should be stress free become stressful.

Note: *The surest route to financial independence that is*

sus- tained over time is personal & spiritual growth & development tied to a plan of action.

Brian Tracey States 5 Reasons why people do not become Wealthy

1. It never occurs to them that its possible for them
2. They never decide to
3. Procrastination
4. The inability to delay gratification
5. Lack of time perspective

"Some people look at the price of moving forward but don't look at the cost of standing still" Unknown

1% of the population earns 96% of the income earned

Poor people only invest $7.50 per year on themselves for personal development.

1:30 ratio/explain

Most adults only get 1 hour of education to every 30 hours of entertainment. It is very simple to change this ratio with minor adjustments in our daily disciplines. It is unheard of to change this ration overnight but incrementally adding more education will drastically alter the course of your life and those you love, hence altering the trajectory of your finances.

"The average person will retire with a $25,000.00 net worth"

You must invest in yourself by learning how to earn money. This means you will spend money on information, books and/or cours- es. Remember you will always get the best return when you invest in yourself.

Although money is a means it does not enhance the skill of

earning money. Earning money; is a skill and it's a learnable skill. Money earned ethically is a byproduct of value creation, and then comes a demand for that value. So in order to sharpen your skills in earning money you must first add value to yourself, create value for others, and then monetize the value through labor, or products and ser- vices.

Most people are only familiar with the most common path to earning money, which is to *trade time for money* (**A Job**). Let's reflect for a moment on the current work that you are doing
If you have ever witnessed someone getting laid off or fired, what is the first thing you hear? Most times its blame towards the com- pany, unfairness, lack of appreciation, but you rarely hear someone say that they were no longer valuable to the company. If you are a business owner with staff and someone is not performing pro- ductively, would you keep them and continue to lose money and eventually close the doors? That is exactly what happens when a person becomes dead weight to a company. This perspective is hard to understand because most folks have never been on the other side of the equation as the owner or even the manager of a
company. Before becoming a business owner, I was judgemental of companies that let people go or made cuts until faced with finan- cial challenges myself. Another outlook is to see a Job as trading *Value* for *Value*. The value you give to a company is your time, energy and skills, while they provide value to you in the form of compensation, structure and a sense of security. Your financial security can only happen when you are intentional about become more valuable. There is a way to avoid being replaced or lessen the chance by keeping up with any changes, plans for growth and cuts that may affect you or your department. You can plan accordingly, learn new skills that are needed for the change and therefore stand out as a person that will add value to the company and not just take up space. The average person will leave this task up to the company, not you right!

Take total responsibility for your economic future and you will stand out. Here are some other things to think about with tradi- tional employment. As employees most people will fall into the 40/40/40 plan, work 40 hours a week for 40 years and retire on 40% of what they were earning. Surprisingly not one of their expenses will decrease to 40% of what they were currently paying. That is why today there are so many retired individuals that work to afford basic expenses. Don't be fooled when an individual past retirement age says they returned to work because they were board at home, truth is- income was needed. Traditional work while honorable has many limits as it relates to earning potential and flexibility.

While it's the most common here are some limits:

- Earning potential based on industry standard
- Set compensation, whether hourly, salary or commission
- Taxed before you receive your paycheck
- Limited security- industry obsolescence (pagers, cd's/ play- ers, traditional marketing)
- Positional leadership instead of influential leadership (ref. John Maxwell/ 5 Levels Of Leadership)

Golden Nugget: 80% of success in anything in your life is psychol- ogy 20% is mechanics.

Questions to Ponder: How do you increase your income? Is it possible to increase your income? *OF COURSE IT IS!*

A few alternative ways of earning money:

- **RROT- Re-Occurring Return On Time**
- **Royalties from music, movies, tv, books, etc.**
- **Passive Income, e.g. (Real Estate)**
- **Residual Income (Direct Sales)**
- **Short and Long-term investments (Stocks,**

Bonds, Real Estate, Yourself, Business)

- Quality referrals/ Finders fees, R.E agents, commissions and other sales

- Membership Initiatives

Be careful with people's mis-conception of sales and the indus- tries connected to the aforementioned income generators. Peo- ple stay away from what they don't understand or they assume the reality and/or challenges when they never did it and then pass that belief on to others.

If these alternative or additional ways to earn money exist, why do the average individual never earn in these ways?

The average person never learn about the **_Law of Compensation_** which states that the amount of money you make is always going to be in exact ratio with:

1. The need for what you do
2. Your ability to do it
3. The difficulty there is in replacing you

Simply ask yourself is there a great need for what I do, and then began to direct your attention on point 2. Continue to develop and refine your skill to do what you do. Every day make a personal commitment to get a little better than the day before. Study the best in your area of expertise and if possible gain mentorship from someone willing to help you decrease your learning curve. Get
on the path of excellence and develop a reputation for speed and dependency and your future will have fortune in it.

When you are generous to others God will up the ante on your financial needs. Once you are financially blessed and have more options it's not an indication that you can now be selfish to others. Adopt an attitude of generosity before you have all that you need and more opportunities will present themselves to you. Once you are clear about how to best utilize your time you will quickly see how it is possible to earn multiple streams of income. There are also others who have gone before you. Don't be so proud that you are not willing to learn from someone else. Many people will die poor because they are not willing to learn from someone else. No man is an island and there is not 1 millionaire that is self-made. They had help! Let's be clear though, they were self-determined, self-motivated, self-starters and they had to make a decision to do whatever it took to become millionaires.

Stats to Ponder: Documented Millionaires By 1900/ 5000 Millionaires
By 1950/ 100,000 Millionaires By 1980/ 1,000,000 Millionaires By 1990/ 2,000,000 Millionaires By 2000/ 7,000,000 Millionaires By 2010/ 10,000,000 Millionaires

Proverbs 8:18-21

"With me are riches and honor, enduring wealth and prosperity. My fruit is better than fine gold; what I yield surpasses choice sil- ver. I walk in the way of righteousness, along the paths of justice, bestowing wealth on those who love me and making their treasur- ies full."

Today in 2014 who knows the number of millionaires that exists. Is it possible to add your name to the total count, Why Not? While in my study time I came across some information that was discussing the number of immigrants that come to the USA and become millionaires while those who are born here never get there big break or miss out on the American Dream. The creative mind kicked in and I began to explore titles to turn into talks, and I came up with *"Rich Immigrant, Poor Citizen"*. 80 % of Ameri- ca's Millionaires are first generation, which simply means they did not inherit or win their millions. Some of the biggest companies in the country were started by folks who are not born in America. Did you know that one of the founder's of Google is an immigrant from the Soviet Union and their company has changed the world of information, creating thousands of millionaires in the process all while in their 20's? Did you know that there are 5 basic ways that people become millionaires?

They are:

1. 74% of millionaires are entrepreneurs/business owners

2. 10% are senior executives of large companies that they helped grow

3. The top 5-10% in a particular field that become the very best and earn accordingly

4. 5% of millionaires are top sales men and women

5. which then invest part of their earnings

Only 1% of millionaires are made up of lottery winners, entertainers, athletes, inventors and authors

Did You Know

- A high % of athletes go broke after 2 years of leaving their sport
- 80% of lottery winners are flat broke after 2 years
- Countless celebrities earn millions of dollars and end up broke, sometimes filing bankruptcy and ending up in jail for tax evasion.

The following scripture tells you why

Proverbs 17;16

"Of what use is money in the hand of a fool, since he has no desire to get wisdom."

2nd Corinthians 9:10/11

"Now he who supplies seed to the sower and bread for food will also supply and increase your store of seed and will enlarge the harvest of your righteousness. You will be made rich in every way so that you can be generous on every occasion, and through us your generosity will result in thanksgiving to God."

Become the biggest GIVER and watch what happens to your life

Chapter Reflections

List 3 Things about your Perspective that has changed as it re- lates to the F-Diamond.

_____
_____
_____

_____

How will you use it to better your life and the lives of others?

_____
_____
_____

Life
Love
Listening
Learning
Laughter

Chapter III

L-Diamond

Love- a profoundly tender, passionate affection for another person. A feeling of warm personal attachment, as for a parent, child, or friend.

Laughter- an inner quality, mood, disposition etc., suggestive of laughter; mirthfulness. An expression or appearance of merriment or amusement.

Listening- to give attention with an ear; attend closely for the pur- pose of hearing. To pay attention; heed; obey.

Learning- knowledge acquired by systematic study in any field of scholarly application. The act or process of acquiring knowledge of skill.

Life- the animate existence or period of animate existence of an indi- vidual; the general or universal condition of human existence.

Love

1st Corintians 13:13

"And now these three remain: Faith, Hope and Love. But the greatest of these is Love.

"Love is like oxygen to the human soul" Tony Robbins

"When you feed your heart & spirit you build and strengthen your courage". If you are living with a fulfilled heart and an unbreakable spirit then life is taken on with courage and chance. Why, because a healthy heart and a renewed spirit will allow an individual to manifest any and every desired result they want in their life. On a daily basis you should give your heart a reason to keep on beating."

Proverbs 19:22

"What a man desires is unfailing Love; better to be poor than a liar.

The most powerful of all emotions

When a baby is first born they need human connection and to be touched by their parents. Babies can actually die if that kinesthet- ic connection and Love is absent. How powerful is that to know. Imagine the affects on adults who are missing that part of the jour- ney. Imagine the many people missing it because they fear losing it, so they protect themselves by never getting close to anyone because they are afraid of losing Love. I can't imagine a life with no Love and closeness to anyone after experiencing the Love of my wife and children. If you find lack in this area and want that great feeling you must first look in the mirror and ask the tough question- do I show love to people, or, do I show love to my fami- ly? Make sure you don't show Love at the office and go home and be- come hateful and angry towards those close to you. Be honest with yourself and if you've never felt the Love of your mother or father work extremely hard to change that with your chil- dren. It sounds simple but these become generational habits and because it's automatic we call it normal. I know siblings who don't speak because it's easier to be upset and angry, sometimes for years. I also know men and women who barely communicate with their parents and unknowingly they pass the abnormal behavior to their children. Even if they speak to their own children at some point in life their children will easily disconnect from loved ones.

Romans 12:10

"Love one another with brotherly affection [as members of one family], giving precedence and showing honor to one another."

***Reference Material:* Rhonda Byrne author of *"The Secret"* (law of attraction) wrote another phenomenal book title "The Pow- er" (Love).**

The biggest takeaway for me in this book is that it shows how liv- ing in the spirit of Love on every level of your life will allow you to attract anything into your life that you DESIRE, but only with the right intentions.

Many people neglect Self-Love and look for Love in so many external things. I'm talking about a healthy, pure and unapolo- getic love for who you are. When you accept the color of your skin, the texture of your hair, your eyes, height, ethnicity, size and every aspect of how God created you, an amazing thing will take place in your life. The limits are now removed from your life because self-image is more important than intellect, creativity and skill. Re- flect for a moment on that point if you disagree. Imagine someone with the highest possible I.Q. and a poor self-image, artistic cre- ative ability and they hate their ethnicity, ability to speak well but always saw failure in their family and therefore see themselves in that manner. It is almost impossible to draw from what they have because a negative self-image is like being locked up while free.

"Human love is selfish, God's love is agape"

Let's talk about self-esteem for this part. Did you know that two out of three people have low self-esteem? How many people are in and out of broken relationships always seeming to miss the mark on true relational happiness? When someone's self-esteem is neg- ative they will except less than what they deserve because every connection to others becomes an attempt to complete them-selves. If someone gets love and acceptance from an abusive person and their self-image is so low they feel like no one else will love them, staying is the best option. Love, whether good or bad will make people function in dysfunction unless there is a positive self-im- age. To clarify, self-image is how you see yourself and how you think others see you, while self-esteem is how you feel internally about yourself. They are hard to separate which is why I use them interchangeably in the content. To continue the point every rela- tionship is limited because of poor self-esteem, from the workplace to school to church. With low self-esteem a person will not take risks and live life to the fullest. Your comfort zone will be to play it safe because you are afraid to fail in front of people. Ask yourself the question, how do I see myself, how do I feel about ME, do I love and define who I am or do I give that task to everyone else?

Began to live your life in a way that others compliment and add to your life but they are not needed to complete you. If you don't, you can become a prisoner of constant reassurance from others and be taken advantage of because they recognize your need for their as- surance. First, you must assess where you are. How would you rate yourself and what will it take to improve your Self-Image/Esteem/ Love. Second, except yourself, stop comparing yourself to others and start taking action on something you're passionate about and when you make progress, celebrate shortly because it boosts your confidence, which feeds positive Self Image/Esteem/Love.

If you neglect emotional maturity it can be your biggest downfall. Your emotions will either contribute to your life or embarrass you. In creating a lecture on EMOTIONS titled "Emotions Make the World Go Around" there are 3 keys areas that I cover and they are Emotional Maturity, Emotional Intelligence and Emotional Re- sponses. Your responses will be based on maturity and intelligence. I highlight the fact that emotional intelligence does not come from academic accomplishments neither does emotional maturity come from age or experience. You must be intentional about gaining a better perspective about your emotions. Emotions can be under-rat- ed especially when we are not intentional and we allow our emo- tions to act on auto-pilot mode. Auto-pilot is dangerous because we respond based on how we feel at that moment. Can you recall any situations in your personal lives that you said something out of anger and then said, "I shouldn't have said that", or you act physically in an intense moment and later deal with consequences that could have been avoided if you took a pause and thought it through?

Love for what you do

"Fall in love with small and big will be attracted to you" Eric Thomas

1st John 3:18(Amp)

"Little children, let us not love [merely] in theory or in speech but
in deed and in truth (in practice and in sincerity"

"When you put your mind to something you really love, never stop trying" Nalani J. Hall (My 8 year old daughter)

You give your best not because you need to impress people. You give your best because that's the only way to enjoy your work". Andrew Matthews

Proverbs 20;13

"Do not love sleep or you will grow poor; stay awake and you will have food to spare".

New life only comes from labor. (elaborate)

Excellence is easier to accomplish in the current work that you do when you truly Love what you do. If not in your current work, think about something that you Love to do so much that you would do it for free. When you love the task at hand your effort is height- ened and it never feels like work. There is also a sense of personal fulfillment when you love and enjoy your work. It is easier to gain promotion or advancement when you pour into your work and go the extra mile. This is hard to do when you have no personal connection to the work that you do. A paycheck alone is no com- parison to passion and love for the work that you may find yourself doing long after retirement age has passed. This is why so many people that transitioned out of traditional employment became entrepreneurs to work within their purpose also known as a calling. That work that you can never escape because it's close to the heart, stirs up the soul and puts a smile on your face.

"You can excel with very little experience, provided you have a very large heart." Kobi Yamada

Proverbs 21:21

"He who pursues righteousness and love finds life, prosperity and
honor."

Love of The wrong things:

1st Corinthians 13:6/7

"It does not rejoice at injustice and unrighteousness, but rejoices when right and truth prevail. Love bears up under everything that comes, is ever ready to believe the best of every person, its hopes are fadeless under all circumstances, and it endures everything without weakening."

As you strive to live the best life possible make sure you don't fall in love with things that are a detriment to your life including peo- ple. Choose habits and fun activities that enrich your life and make you feel good about yourself. Remember that the

emotion of Love is not bias or prejudice, it's as powerful and influential whether directed towards something good or bad, a positive friend or a neg- ative friend that drain you. Most of us never recognize that the hin- drances in life that slow us down and stunt our growth are things we will not let go because we love them. This is seen in every
area of life from self-destructive habits and behaviors to abusive relationships that have lead to death in some cases. Let's get better at defining who and what we Love and ask one simple question: What is this contributing to my life? If the answer is a definitive nothing, then maybe you have a false sense of love for that particu- lar thing. We are all guilty or have been guilty of loving something that is not good for us, even if that something is the foods we eat. An unhealthy diet will affect you over time, not immediately, while toxic relationships will not push you off of a cliff, but it will nudge you way off course and eventually off of the cliff.

Proverbs 15:17

"Better a meal of vegetables where there is Love, than a fattened calf with hatred."

An emotion that many people struggle with is anger, the opposite of love. Anger feels strong for the moment so you must be careful that you don't trick yourself when you're angry and call it strength.
This reality is a hindrance for many people. There is an aspect of anger that is productive and shows strength when the anger
prompts you to take action on something that gets a positive result. A lot of the community work that I do today was birthed out my concern and anger about what was happening in my community and others like mine around the country. So remember that healthy anger is productive and unhealthy anger is self-destructive, with a domino effect on anyone connected to the angry individual. Some- times we as human beings dealing with our human nature become angry because

of life's circumstances or actions against us by others, which is why we must always asses how we treat others es- pecially friends and family. We may love them but act in a manner rooted in anger. Anger will also make you treat strangers a certain way and rob you of new, fresh and healthy relationships. Become aware of what we get angry about and determine that others will not be subjected to it.

"A woman that is her own Goliath will also be her mans Goliath" <u>David G. Evans</u>

In this quote the same is also true of a man who is his own Goli- ath. Look at your own life and be sure that you do not sabotage your own happiness, relationships and success because if you do, it will be easy to sabotage the lives of others. Watch the words that you say about yourself. If you call yourself a failure, you will act like a failure and treat others like they are failures. Substitute the word failure with any word that you use to describe yourself and the same applies. We project it on our children, friends and family. From this point make a vow to yourself to listen to the opinion of you that matter and listen to your own words when they are posi- tive and reflect the best you possible. You are a work in progress, remember that!

<u>*Proverbs 16:6*</u>

"Through love and faithfulness sin is atoned for; through the fear of the Lord a man avoids evil." _____

Imitate the Love & Humility of Christ

Phillipians 2:1-5

"If you have any encouragement from being united with

Christ, if any comfort from his love, if any fellowship with the spirit, if any tenderness and compassion, then make my joy complete by being like-minded, having the same love, being one in spirit and purpose. Do nothing out of selfish ambition or vain conceit, but in humility consider others better than yourselves. Each of you should look not to your own interests, but also to the interests of others."

"In life we are made by those who love us and by those who re- fuse to love us" John Powell

Joel 2:13

"Rend your heart and not your garments. Return to the Lord your God, for he is gracious and compassionate, slow to anger and abounding in Love, and he relents from sending calamity."

Learn

The worst advice is great advice that you never act on!

"The mind is everything; what you think you become" Buddha

Before diving into this section lets change how we view our mind. I want to broaden your perspective of your greatest asset, YOUR MIND! Typically we think of our mind as a tool that we use for school to solve problems or in life to think through situations
that we face. While this is true it imposes a great limit on the real potential of our mind. Make this small adjustment and view your mind as a mental muscle and like our bodies physical muscle needs developing so does your mind(mental muscle). There is a differ- ence in seeing your mind as a tool to use for its limited purpose, like a saw that cuts wood or a hammer that bangs in nails than see- ing it as a mental muscle which allows you to be intentional about developing it. Most of us only use about 10%

of our minds real potential, which equates to the sum total of where we are in life.

Those who develop, strengthen and constantly grow their mind(- mental muscle) will achieve more, contribute more and have a different quality of life than those who don't. A child's mind is able to learn four different languages because of their curiosity, capacity to learn and lack of mental corruption that limits most adults. The mind is so powerful that if we use up to 50% of our true mental potential we could learn 40 different languages.

"The illiterate of the 21st century will not be those who cannot read and write, but those who cannot learn, unlearn and re- learn." Alvin Toffler

Once you make a decision to become a life-long learner you will get golden nuggets from many sources. While walking my daugh- ter to school on one of the coldest days in the past two years, we were engaged in our morning ritual of sharing. A middle aged man was digging through the trash and my daughter was attempting
to rationalize why he was in the trash. She said "he's looking for furniture for his apartment" "he's looking for something to sell to get some food". I began to discuss gratitude and being appreciative for what you have then I shared an old quote "one man's trash is another man's treasure". Her response was "from your mouth to God's ears". This was profound to me being a lover of great quotes and positive insight. I asked her where she got that from and she said one of my movies. I'm sure the movie had plenty of conver- sations but she remembered "from your mouth to God's ears".

Maybe it was the timing that made it resonate the way it did. In that moment she was the teacher. That morning was confirmation that kids can exhibit wisdom, so spend some time listening to your children they may inspire your next business idea or the key to your next promotion. It's no accident that she is co-authoring the children's version of this book.

"The person who can read and don't is no better that the person who can't read, and sometimes worse" Unknown

Golden Question

"If a person buys a $10,000,000 home with a library in it, did they buy it because of the library in it or were they able to buy it because of their library?" Jim Rohn

Key Point to Remember: Your most valuable **ASSET** is your **earning ability**, while your most valuable **TOOL** to increase it, is your **learning ability**. Learning should always lead to earning when it's properly applied and adds value.

Confucius Quote:

"Tell me, and I will forget, show me, and I may remember, in- volve me, and I will understand".

Today make a personal commitment to become a life-long learn- er.

Do you think a person could be extremely brilliant and not get the best results? You better believe it. Remember that common sense doesn't equal common practice. What's easy to do is also easy not to do. The obvious thing that will get better results will elude most people. I was at a conference and the gentleman training said that "people come from around the world to America looking for an op- portunity, while folks in America never take advantage of the many opportunities all around them everyday". In my youth I used to be puzzled at the number of individuals who come here and in a few years they achieve great success. Sometimes, speaking no English, but having a strong desire to learn and achieve. In my ignorance
I listened to all the people who never quite made it. They always made excuses for their lack of success and said things like, foreign- ers get all the loans from banks, they came here with money, get help from the government and other nonsense. Truth is, they were

willing to work hard, delay gratification, unite and share resources with others from their country. They practiced a Kwanzaa princi- ple (Ujamaa) also called *Collective Economics*. The irony is their willingness to accept employment that folks born here were not willing to accept for whatever reason, and within a few years they are business and home owners. They took the time to learn the language and how the economics of this country worked. Those of us who live here never take that time to learn a second language or the economics of our own country, therefore achieve less than someone new to America. This also applies to very educated Americans who never make it to financial independence.

Food For Thought:

Every $1.00 you spend on personal development, learning and getting better will yield $30.00 to your bottom line. When I first stumbled across this principle, I measured it in my own life. To my surprise, each book, class or training I invested in, always yielded a return of 30x or more to my bottom line, but only when I took action. This principle does not apply just because you pur- chase a self help book or home-study course.

"I will study and get ready, and someday my chance will come." Abraham Lincoln

Process of Learning

- *Information Intake*
- *Process & Filtering*
- *Proper Application to better your life and the lives of others*
- *Unlearn and Shift Paradigms*

Learning does not come naturally for everyone. Reflect on your life and try to recall the times that you repeated the same mistake over and over again and expected different results, some call it in- sanity. Many people assume that information alone is all they need to learn, but without the other three aforementioned steps, it's just information.

The best way to learn anything new is to first try and make sure you give it your all. As a life-long learner you should see learning as the water to your soil of potential. Soil is the birthplace of beau- tiful flowers, fruits, vegetables, minerals and other vital materials that human survival depends on. So, it's safe to say that learning *(water)* will unleash the unlimited potential *(soil)* within you and bring forth ideas, projects, inventions, innovation in your industry and medical breakthroughs. Learning should never feel like a task or hard work.

Treat learning like a skill, which means you must get better at it. Effective learning calls on a different way of thinking. If most peo- ple said what they were thinking, they would be speechless. Most people are on auto-response somewhat like a car on cruise control. Not to belittle or to discredit any human being but reflect on the times when your response was in a particular way just because you heard someone else respond that way or saw something on television and we know that television will allow you to get lost
in someone else's reality. Without proof or evidence of its validity, we pass on the response to others as truth and on and on it goes.
Always find truth in what you say and be honest when you don't know because the learning starts there, in that moment of humil- ity. Think, process and gather your thoughts before you respond. In building new relationships always learn about and get to know people before you buy into someone's opinion of them. Don't cheat yourself in life because it's easier to be on auto-response. I know it takes less effort and work to be on auto-response, but what is the accumulated cost of the relationships and opportunities lost, perhaps thousands, maybe

millions!

What is your learning style?

Write your Answer/Response: _____

If you don't know, welcome to the club. The average person does not know what their learning style is. As a matter of fact, our public school system has not figured out how to affectively educate students with different learning styles. As an educator I am always looking for ideas to better educate the community I serve, which
is primarily African-American and Latino. In the area of helping youth and young adults escape the cycle of juvenile justice and the adult prison system, I began to research why the system thrived. In my studies I came across a phenomenal book by Jawanza Kunjufu "How to Keep Black Boys Out of Special Education". It suggests some serious questions to the educational system, policy makers and government agencies focused on education. He points out the variation of learning styles, gender learning differences and cultur- al differences in learning. The current system only caters to 1 or 2 styles and hardly ever considers cultural and/or gender differences. Because of this bias every student's ability to learn is based on those few methods deemed the best by the educational system. The amount of males in special education is twice as high as females.
Studies were done to look at cognitive development, mem- ory, attention span, mathematical equations and other areas. Students in special education were able to grasp usually hard concepts and solve problems when the use of different meth- ods catering to other learning styles was used to teach the class. Kids from urban com- munities were able to learn the latest hip-hop/rap song verbatim, but received low grades in subjects that required memory and cognitive ability. The ques- tion becomes do we need more special education or training for educators on different learning styles.
What do you think? Are there areas in your life where you felt

in- adequate or incapable of learning something, so the default was to give up? In order to get the best from the rest of your life you have to understand this about yourself and those you teach. I am con- stantly reminding my children that although we want them to get good grades, that they are not their grade. I have witnessed young people who see themselves as a failure because of the grade they got on a test. I have also witnessed the cruelty of kids who tease and sometimes bully kids who are placed in special education or remedial classes. Let's become aware of this reality as we navigate our own children through the education maze to help them live the best quality of life. **My** daughter is now an eighth grader and this point became very clear just a few weeks ago as we were talking at the dinner table. She was discussing her experience in seventh grade with a teacher that she was not to fond of. The typical response to the child would be "the teacher is not there to be liked or to be your friend" but instead I let her explain. "Well I did terrible in science last year
but so did most of the class". Almost everyone failed except for a few students that got a C-. Although her and my wife discussed his teaching style, I was outside of the loop that year so the topic was new to me. When she described his method of teaching science
it was very limited; he would show a video, give an assign- ment out of the book then test them at the end of the week. Not much engagement with the students, no demonstrations, exhibits or in depth explanations of concepts. Before she began the eighth grade school year she said I hate science I don't get it. She is getting A's now in the eighth grade due to the difference in the method of the
teachers. My daughter was able to articulate the difference in meth- od and no longer had doubt in her ability to learn sci- ence. The way the traditional school system work is they grade the kid on ability to learn and performance, while the problem could very well be the method in which the teacher instructs. Due to this realization by my daughter it also made her aware of her learning style and once you know your learning style

you can also be intentional about in- creasing your ability to learn in other ways. Now my daughter can affectively learn from any teacher.

Which of these styles apply to you?

Learning Styles According to: Dr. Howard Gardener

- Linguistic learners
- Logical/ Mathematical learners
- Spatial learner
- Body/Kinesthetic
- Musical learner
- Interpersonal learner
- Intrapersonal learner

Which of these styles apply to you?

Discuss these styles with your peers and write down how they feel about each:

Process & Filtering Typical feelings

- Comfort
- Dis-comfort
- Confident
- Unaware/Lost

How do you build on your style with this new awareness and also have an understanding of the others?

Become a professional problem solver and by default you'll add value to those whose problems you solve. Types of Problems you can solve: *Personal, Social and Systemic*

Note: When you're intentional about solving problems at work and in business the favor of God will fall on your life. This will only happen when you go above and beyond the required learning for the job. Learn to be the best at your job then learn the job of those you report too.

Many people confuse mental activity with thinking. What if you had confirmation that the mind is the greatest power in all creation? Would you respect it more and monitor its deposits, of course you would, at least you should? If your arms and legs were taken away from you and you had the full functioning capacity of your brain you can still become wealthy and create scientific breakthroughs.

In life people are not financially poor from poor working habits because most people work hard, sometimes having two and three jobs. In fact it comes from poor thinking habits. The mind has an amazing way of conforming to what everyone else is doing or what others suggest we should do if it is not stretched through thinking and creating.

"As a Man Thinketh" by James Allen should be required reading for companies trying to grow and for students, especially male. *"As a Woman Thinketh"* is also available.

Proverbs 14;33

"Wisdom reposes in the heart of the discerning and even among fools she lets herself be known"

Proper Application to improve your life and the lives of others Pre-Frontal Cortex which is the executive part of the brain
- Forethought
- Judgment
- Organization
- Planning

YOU *must become aware of all of the mental faculties of the brain to become better in every area of your life, they are:*

- ✓ Perception
- ✓ Will
- ✓ Memory
- ✓ Imagination
- ✓ Reason
- ✓ Intuition

Each of these is different mental muscles to build and strengthen like physical muscles.

They are also life building tools. If you see your mental fac- ulties like a hammer, saw, measuring tape etc., you can use the best tool for the task or assignment at hand.

Proverbs 4; 7-9

Wisdom is supreme: therefore get wisdom

Though it cost you all you have, get understanding

Esteem her and she will exalt you; embrace her and she will honor you.

She will set a garland of grace on you head, And present you with a crown of splendor.
Unlearn and Shift Paradigms

I can recall when I read a phenomenal book titled "**Think and Grow Rich** by Napolean Hill. This was actually the first book that launched my personal development journey over 15 years ago.
There is no dollar amount that will equate to the value brought to my life from that book and every book that followed. There was a particular section that talked about the difference between general knowledge and specialized knowledge. The point was highlight- ing the danger of specialized knowledge, which you obtain mostly through some form of higher education i.e., colleges, universities, medical school or law school. This is during a time when higher education was sold as the surest road to the American Dream. With specialized knowledge all of your energy was focused on 1 skill and in 1 industry. The common belief was that these industries would be around forever so job security was the ultimate goal. Fast forward and today many students are holding college degrees that have very little value and many times have a tough time finding work in the industry they studied. Recent studies show that college debt has surpassed credit card debt and students are taking whatev- er work they can find to try to put a dent in massive debt from their pursuit of the American Dream.

I am an advocate of education but we must do a better job of building awareness for young people about their higher education pursuits and to look closely at the emerging industries to avoid the pitfall of those becoming obsolete. I was watching a documentary called "The Crisis of Education", to my surprise it was not about students but about the professors. There is this large population of highly educated professors called adjunct professors who are only hired as part-time professors. Community colleges and smaller schools normally use adjunct professors but the larger schools are doing away with full-time positions and tenure and leveraging them to lessen the budget and have no obligation to offer benefits. This current crisis has many highly degreed educators having to be at 2 or 3 schools to make a decent living and many accessing government assistance and food stamps to survive.

Career changes are prevalent amongst this group even those with Doctorate and PHd's. As great as specialized knowledge is, see how crippling it can be if your industry or the need within the industry changes and you are left with extensive debt and no other skills or abilities.

The only way to expand your capacity in life is to continue learning on a daily basis. There is no such thing as an insignifi- cant improvement.

The old adage states that when the student is ready the teacher will appear

- **Adopt the motto of being 90% Student and 10% Teacher/Educator**

    If you spend most of your time learning and growing then when you are in the capacity of a teacher/educator you will give quality and substantive information and insight to others.

- **You are not responsible for someone who does not take your advice.**

    If you give someone relevant and useable advice and they choose not to use it and miss an opportunity or suffer a setback you should never blame yourself. The choice was made by them.

- **Become a deliberate thinker and not a reactionary thinker.**
    Make a decision to be solution driven and always think on purpose about situations and problems that arise. Don't focus on problems but have readily available solutions and see yourself as a creative problem solver. This helps you stay productive and raises your value to employers, organi- zation and to your own endeavors and ventures.

- Increase your center of awareness which will enhance one of your best internal tools, discernment.

Continuing to learn will ultimately increase your awareness and understanding, therefore shaping your responses and decision making. Your internal intelligence will get better. Call it your soul, spirit or discernment!

Jim Rohn: "Let the past become a teacher instead of a burden"

Half Truths: Statements that we live by

- 1. Knowledge is power
- 2. What you don't know won't hurt you
- 3. Don't sweat the small stuff
- 4. Practice makes perfect
- 5. Ignorance is bliss
- 6. Repetition is the mother of learning
- 7. Money is the root of all evil
- 8. No pain no gain
- 9. This relationship is 50/50 (percentage)

The Other Half: What was left out

- 1. Knowledge is only information until properly applied to better your life and the lives of others. Knowl- edge should never be used for manipulation or deception because you have it and someone else *doesn't. People today are drowning in information but starving for mean- ing.*

➢ *2. If you don't know something that is imperative to a critical or life-changing decision, that can and will hurt you. Sometimes what you know will also hurt you because common-sense does not always lead to common- practice. The measure of poverty and wealth is what you don't know.*

➢ *3. Much of life is about the small stuff that we take for granted. Appreciation and gratitude is small but sig- nificant. Sending a handwritten Thank You Note is small but it's remembered by the recipient. Live life like every- thing matters because it does. Excellence in small things leads to a life of significance.*

➢ *4. Perfection is an illusion. Practice only makes you more efficient, effective and productive. Athletes or other professionals who are considered the best in their sport or industry practice harder once they are labeled the best. True mastery only happens when you never arrive always striving to get better, but never perfect.*

➢ *5. Ignorance is not bliss, Ignorance is poverty. Igno- rance is heartache. Ignorance is pain and suffering. The other perspective is a little different, huh.*

➢ *6. What about people who function in dysfunction or become conditioned for crisis, in other words what if you're repeating the wrong thing and you're con- vinced that it's the right thing, something to think about.*

➢ *7. Refer to the good book, it says the love of mon- ey is the root of all evil. Society has a way of demon- izing those with money. Those who built wealth the right way do not love money, they love time freedom*

& choices. Remember money will only magnify who you are, good or bad. Earn as much as you can, support your family and give back in proportion to your accumulated wealth. Money is Okay and if you don't believe me, go to the gas station with a good attitude and try to fill up your tank….. Exactly!

- *8. This statement applies depending on the context, but there are times when we as human beings intro- duce self-inflicted pain because we ignore the warn- ing signs or accept the wrong counsel/advice. With enough condition- ing some folks suffer a life-time of pain and never experi- ence the gains, just a thought.*

- *9. If a person is bringing anything less than 100% of themselves there may be a problem. 100% assumes total responsibility and also diminishes the thought of someone fixing or completing you and vice-versa. Stop seeking validation from those that need valida- tion. You are a whole individual, just a thought!*

Proverbs 18;2

"A fool finds no pleasure in understanding, but delights in airing his own opinions."

Point to remember: **If and when you doubt yourself and the pow- er of your mind know that the brain functions at 4 Bil- lion activ- ities per minute**

"Education is the most powerful weapon which you can use to change the world" Nelson Mandela

Laughter

Do you believe the old adage "Laughter is good for the soul"

"You must enjoy life and not just endure it" **Joel Osteen**

Fact: **Smiling only takes 13 muscles, while a frown takes 110 muscles!**

There are some surgeons that will not operate on a patient if they have a negative mental attitude about the operation and the out- come. Or, if they feel that they will not make it through the oper- ation. I once heard a story of a person who was terminally ill and was given a short time to live. Determined to live and make the most of the rest of her life, the woman decided to fill her days with laughter by watching funny movies and spending quality time with her family. This time of joy and laughter did something amazing for the sick woman. Her joy and laughter became her strength and internal medicine. Sickness began to leave her body and to the doctors amazement she became healed of what was killing her. **Reference the** *"Happiness Advantage by John Anchor"* It is scientifically proven that Happiness is a choice.

Happiness gives you a great advantage for your entire life and the lives of those around you.

The minute you smile Dopeamine is activated in your brain and you feel better.

90% of your long term happiness is determined by your view of the world (perspective)

Proverbs 14;13

"Even in laughter the heart may ache, and joy may end in grief"

Is it possible to be celebrating a proud & joyful moment and face adversity & difficulty at the same time? If so, what gets your atten- tion? How do you focus on getting better results and being produc- tive when you're faced with a crisis that causes emotional turmoil?

What if we looked at our laughter as seeds to a life of joy? I've witnessed people who are going through something in their life watch a movie that is either depressing or works in partnership with what they are faced with. Negative news gets your attention or being around those going through the same thing, which is not bad if they are working to feel better and get back to a place of joy.
The reality is that many people find it easier to have a pity party or just complain about what they're dealing with. Recognize the problem, work towards a solution and do things that you find joy in. Watch something funny, play with your children, exercise, read
a motivating story. There is no one size fits all approach but believe me laughter will always affect you internally and externally.

Reference "Pursuit of Happiness"

Proverbs 15;30

A cheerful look brings joy to the heart, and good news gives health to the bones.

Humor comes from the Latin word Homar- which means to be
flexible and fluid

What makes childhood so wonderful is the fact that kids on aver- age will laugh 50 times per day to adults 2 times per day. Children find joy in the simplest things that life has to offer, while many adults seek perfection, chase their dreams and work tirelessly only to retire with very little joy and peace of mind.

**"*A change of feeling is a change of destiny" Neville*

Listen

Be a selective listener depending on the circumstances. You have to be careful who you allow to dump **any** and **everything** into your mental factory or who you allow to plant negative seeds into the rich **soil** called your **mind.**

Proverbs 15:31

"He who listens to a life-giving rebuke will be at home among the wise"

Proverbs 1:28

"Even a fool is thought wise if he keeps silent, and discerning if he holds his tongue"

"Gold there is, and rubies in abundance, but lips that speak knowl- edge are a rare jewel"

Proverbs 19:20

"Listen to advice and accept instruction, and in the end you will be wise"

Effective Communication is two or more people coming together
to find common ground.

- Look for common ground instead of having a turf war
- Be intentional about getting better at listening and when you speak make sure the person is ready and able to receive what you have to share.
- Wisdom from Jim Rohn **"Don't be sloppy with words" "Say it until they get it.**
- It is the responsibility of the person speaking to make sure that the person listening interprets their

words correctly.

- Many people assume that hearing is listening, lis- tening is understanding and understanding is caring. All 4 are different.

- When you engage others instead of being interesting show genuine interest in what they are saying.

Proverbs 3;3

"He who guards his lips guards his life, but he who speaks rashly will come to ruin."

Life

What would you do if you only had three months to live?

How would you treat those around

you? Would you become bitter and

cynical?

Would you reflect on all the mistakes you've made?

Would you reflect on all the accomplishments you've

had? Which feelings would be present regret or fulfillment?

What big goal would you try to achieve?

Is there anyone that you would apologize to or thank for some- thing they did for you?

Who have you never said I Love You to and know you should?

"Our attitude toward life determines life's attitude toward us"
Earl Nightingale

However you answered the previous questions is a reflection of what you should continue doing or an awakening to what you should begin to do. This exercise will be different for everyone but helpful if you wish to live a fulfilling, fruitful and productive life. If you made it this far in this project, I trust that you desire mutual- ly beneficial relationships and goal achievement in your life. I have witnessed countless people who treat themselves better when they are faced with life-threatening circumstances. I also witness people treat friends and family better when they thought life for them was limited for whatever reason. Stop today and assess how you have been treating those you say you love and care about. Who have you not forgiven? We can change the quality of our lives if we just live, love and achieve at the highest level *now*, instead of when it's winding down in the final hour. Don't cheat yourself because others are miserable and don't have to be. You make a decision to work on developing a healthy attitude so that tension can turn into peaceful thoughts and fulfillment towards others. The difference in you will be evident and this will better your chance to live the life you deserve.

"We make a living by what we get, but we make a life by what we
give." Norman MacFinan

"Life is a fight for territory" Les

Brown You Must Protect Your Soil

Character

An Excert from a Book Titled (Character) by: Samuel Smiles (1812)

"To be always intending to live a new life, but never to find time to set about it,---this is as if a man should put off eating and drinking and sleeping from one day to another, until he

is starved and destroyed."

Quality of Life is about living the life you want. That includes those who bring out the best in you. Indulging in the work or en- deavors of your choice, and your ability to make a contribution.

"Those who do not create the future they want must endure the future they get." Draper L. Kaufman, Jr.

Socrates states

"The unexamined life is not worth living"

Proverbs 19;23

"The fear of the Lord leads to life: Then one rests content, untouched by trouble"

Legacy

John F. Kennedy"s Golden Nugget: *"Ask not what your country can do for you, ask what you can do for your country"*
Job 42;10-17

Someone who lives doing Legacy activity everyday will experience pure joy, which is the type of joy that only comes from giving. Any legacy worth remembering was rooted in giving others time, love, energy, resources and more.

Many times in life, pain is the birthplace of a *LEGACY*

Susan Komen (Breast Cancer Foundation) Research her story
and see the pain that inspired her efforts

Facts to consider:

- It's world impact
- The pink movement
- How many industries it has involved
- How much progress have been made towards research and new medicines
- New technologies
- The flow of currency e.g. brands, products, goodwill donations, emerging industries and more
- Almost every professional sport recognize, support and wear the pink ribbon and now you see pink uniforms and footwear
- Investment in early detection has reduced breast cancer mortality by 30%
- Countless organizations have been inspired because her efforts

Persoanal experiences

✓ While making a purchase at Walgreen's before closing the sale the clerk pushed a button and there was an option to add $1.00 to my purchase to donate to Breast Cancer and I did. This one small activity gener- ates Millions of dollars for the foundation, LEGACY

Do you think this story would be worthy of its place in the his- tory books? *You better believe it!* The Pink Ribbon has almost become a world-wide household symbol, with an exception of the countries with no television. <u>*LEGACY!*</u>

"Leave your story better than you found it". <u>M.H.</u>

<u>Ward</u> <u>Psalm 2:7-9</u>
He said to me, "You are my son, today I have become your Father. Ask of me,

And I will make the nations your inheritance, the ends of the earth your possession."

By 2020 the Coca Cola Foundation has a goal to support 5 million women entrepreneurs in an initiative called *"Half The Sky"*

To Summarize the L-Diamond:

(LIVE, PURSUE YOUR DREAMS, DO YOUR BEST, CHERISH, TRAVEL OFTEN, KEEP YOUR PROMISES, LOVE, SAY PLEASE, AND THANK YOU, BELIEVE IN YOURSELF, BE KIND, DO WHAT YOU LOVE, HELP OTHERS, TRY NEW THINGS, LAUGH, SEIZE THE DAY, BE AN INSPIRATION, WORK HARD, PLAY HARDER)

Chapter Reflections

List 3 Things about your Perspective that has changed as it relates to the L-Diamond.

_____
___
_____
_____
_____
___ ___
_____
_____

How will you use it to better your life and the lives of others?

_____
___ ___
_____
_____
___ ___
_____
_____
___ ___
_____

People **Purpose** passione
Persistance perseverance

Chapter IV
P-Diamond

Passion- any powerful or compelling emotion, as love or hate.

People- human beings, as distinguished from animals or any other beings.

(Patience)/Persistence- continued existence or occurence. The continuance of an effect after its cause is gone.

Perseverance- steady persistence in a course of action, a purpose, a state etc., especially in spite of difficulties, obstacles or discourage- ment.

Purpose- the reason for which something exists or is done, made, used etc.

Passion

This has to be the single emotion that acts like fuel to a vehicle. Without the proper fuel in a vehicle it will not run properly or run at all. Passion was the driving force to many great accomplish- ments, breakthroughs in technology and innovative products and services. Passion will make you stay up late and wake up extreme- ly early to find a solution to a problem. Passion will make you do random acts of kindness if there is interest in a person.

There are two parts to passion that I will expound upon for this section. First there is passion that you have for a specific thing, person, issue or cause. The other part is you being a passionate person in your life about whatever is important to you, whether it's important to others or not. There is a difference but they also go to- gether. You can have a particular passion about someone or some- thing but not pursue it with passion. Take for instance when most people fall in love with someone it was because they pursued them with a level of passion but once years have gone by and you settle that passion becomes absent. This also happens to dreams and goals. Sometimes life can kill passion due to work related stress, bad relationships, family issues and a ton of others circumstances.

There is also a large part of our society who are working while miserable because they have not connected their pas- sion to their work. One of my greatest discoveries was when I discovered what I was passionate about but then learning how to pursue it with passion. That passion also transferred to my family and friends and how I treat them every-day, not just when I feel good or when things are going right for me. De- pending on the things that stir your passion, you may also find that a particular job may not sat- isfy that passion. If you do work make sure you enjoy your work, make sure it's some- thing that makes you feel good while doing it. If you have ideas, concepts or creative products, that may be the birthing of a business.

Living life to the fullest will stir your passionate side, but finding passion as it relates to your life's work can be challenging. "***Re- member to Love yourself through the process*** ***D-Math***

Take a few minutes to answer these questions. They may hold the
final number in the combination to unlock a whirlwind of poten- tial.

1. Start by looking a little deeper into your work, job or what you do for income. What do you do and do you enjoy it?

2. Then think about and list the activities that you feel good doing inside and outside of work.

3. How do you view being a contribution to society, is that someone else's job or do you matter?

4. What will you do for free because you enjoy it that much?

5. Think of something you accomplished or did for someone and it made you proud of yourself and you had a great night sleep?

6. What puts a smile on your face and can also bring tears to your eyes?

7. What causes keep you up late and make you pray for a solution or change?

These are **Indicators** in discovering you passion, potential and purpose.

People

"There are three types of people, winners, losers and winners that haven't learned how to win yet" <u>*Les Brown*</u> **God has given us Dominion over all the earth. Nature/Nurture (Man and wild turkeys)**

One late night after a long productive day I was up watching a program on the discovery channel. The program was about a man who was studying the lives of wild turkeys in their natural habitat. His study was done for an extensive period of time. He studied everything from the mating, birthing and social patterns of the wild turkeys. He carefully observed how they communicate, how they migrate and their daily diet. To my amazement was the second segment of the program in which the man would attempt to assim- ilate with the wild turkeys providing the new information gathered during his study. In the beginning of the process his first goal was to be accepted by the wild turkeys. He slept where they slept and would even communicate with them effectively. When they moved he moved. He was totally accepted by the wild turkeys, but there was still another level of assimilation. He took a nest of newly born wild turkeys and would attempt to raise them as their parent. They never laid eyes on their biological mother so he was all they knew. He did everything from feed them to hold and nurture them as their mother. They would respond to his call and everything. He learned the different characteristics of each baby turkey and was specific to their needs like a parent to each child.

I don't know if I was more astonished by his ability to assimilate and gain acceptance from wild turkeys or the human ability to ob- serve, study and become something totally outside of their natural existence. This ability was not given to all of God's creations, only people!

"You can take my business, burn up my buildings, but give

me my people and I'll build the business right back again"
<u>*Henry*</u> <u>*Ford*</u>

As *people* we are the only beings with the gift of the verbal narrative, the ability to communicate with words, in different languages.

Becoming a CHAMPION will bring out the Champion in others. Throughout this material the ultimate goal is to awaken what you already possess, **POTENTIAL**, which is the main ingredient in the Champion recipe. Once your potential is aroused and the Cham- pion is stirred and begins to rise up in you, at that point it's easier to let the sleeping giant out than to try and contain it and settle for mediocrity. Don't fight the natural order of things. The reason life feels so frustrating to those who are not living to their fullest po- tential is because the natural order is *progress, advancement and growth*, not defeat, mediocrity and conformity. Your life will give you all options, but you must decide to follow the natural order and not let a moment of defeat, mediocrity and conformity become life- long circumstances. Whether you know it or not people are watch- ing you and you may be the example they follow, good or bad.

We can do more than belong, we can participate.

*"You will rise by lifting **others**"* Robert Green Ingersoll

Walt Disney said *"You can dream, create, design and build the most wonderful place in the world, but it requires **people** to make the dream a reality.*

No two *people* on planet earth are identical

People are God's highest form of creation
During class at Smart from the Start a young lady stated that she had a desire to start an Escort Service Business. As she shared more I realized her total vision was to have prostitutes with differ- ent types of services for whatever a client desired.

A turning point in the conversation was when she said that she would send her girls to school and make sure they had a good education and help them with housing as well as other essential needs. I could hear that
she had a heart for her potential employees (young prostitutes). My next question was, what other interests do you have? To my surprise she wants to own a home and other businesses. My next question was, if any of the other ideas could earn as much or more would you still consider the escort business? While pondering the question total silence fell over the room. She then stated the reason for her interest in the escort business. After a long pause her eyes began to water as she shared that something happened to her as a child and her mother wasn't there for her and she soon ended up in a life of prostitution. Other class participants began to give com- passionate insight and advice to help her reconsider the idea. One lady asked her what it would do to her if her young daughter came to her one day and said she wanted to be a prostitute. This became a moment of inspiration for the entire class. **"It would crush me"**. **"I was never taught how to be a mother"**. More tears began to flow and she said **"maybe I could help girls that consider that life"**. I said to her that pain is a great source of power if it has the right focus and guidance. As we wrapped up the class she was em- braced by the other participants. This was a moment to be remembered. The human connection in the room was unbelievable. My eyes were a little moist and you know men don't cry, yeah right!
I was so inspired that I had to write and document that experience immediately. Whatever care and love she missed growing up was partly restored that day because of *people* and more importantly, her outlook on life and her self-image had changed.

Quoted in 12 Pillars by Chris Widener & Jim Rohn

People will fall into 3 categories
- Dis-Association

- Limited-Association
- Expanded-Association

"The ability to deal with people is as purchasable a commodity as sugar or coffee" **John D. Rockeller**

Did you know that most people with a problem don't necessarily want to solve the problem? If someone mess around and solve the problem their desire for attention is gone. If the person is conditioned to function in crisis they will go out of their way to create a new crisis or problem to get the attention and fulfill the desire once again. In dealing with people you will also encounter those who will try to inflict pain on you. What do you do when all you've done is good things for someone and for whatever reason they dislike you, hate you or do wrong to you. Sounds crazy but it happens, especially if you make a decision to change some things in your life and start on a new track.

Following Scripture will elaborate this point:

1st Samuel 19:4-5

"Jonathan spoke highly of David to Saul his father and said to him, "Let not the king do wrong to his servant David; he has not wronged you, and what he has done has benifited you greatly. He took his life in his hands when he killed the Phillistine. The Lord won a great victory for all Israel, and you saw it and were glad. Why then would you do wrong to an innocent man like David by killing him for no reason".

"Things that come easy for you may not come easy for someone else, so never look down at them and curse your gift." (elaborate) T.D. Jakes

Perserverence

"You may have a fresh start any moment you choose, for this thing that we call failure is not the falling down, but the staying down." **Mary Pickford**

Develop the quality of being unstoppable, despite what the cir- cumstances look like to the natural eye. It takes a certain type of person with undeniable focus to do it even when there's no evi- dence that the desired results will happen. Be clear and certain that this is when you are moving towards a major goal that suits your major purpose in life. This should also be towards something that gives you joy and personal fulfillment, while it simultaneously helps others.

Imagine living a life where you can sleep when the wind is blowing because you have taken all of the necessary precautions to secure your family, your belongings and your joy and peace
of mind. (scrip. Highlight story of Jesus in the ship"). If you are wondering why I added joy and peace of mind is because many of us give that responsibility to everyone but ourselves. When you persevere during tough economic times or when government is in turmoil or while there is a family crisis, something in you happens that changes your life. Suddenly you realize as my mentor Jim Rohn says "The wind(circumstances of life) blows on us all, you must set a better sail for your life or you'll end up on the rocks shipwrecked". Set your sail for the right destination, no matter the wind. There are those that took control of their lives and I encour- age you to do the same. Learn how to bounce back so that you no longer live like a foam cup on a windy day because it has no control over where it will end up.

Your ability to persevere never depends on how you reach your goals or your destination. To illustrate this imagine two vehi- cles on two separate roads headed somewhere. Vehicle 1 is an old Jelopi on the freeway of success headed in the direction of your goals and dreams. Vehicle 2 is a brand new

Mercedes Benz on a dirt road lost with no direction. Which vehicle would you prefer to be in? WHY!

Most people would say the Mercedes Benz on a dirt road over an old jelopi on the freeway. Because of human nature they will omit the last part and focus on the type of car, ignoring the fact that the Mercedes Benz is on a dirt road lost with no direction and the old jelopi is on the freeway of success headed towards your dreams and goals.

Phillipeans 1;6

"The same God that started this good work, is the same God that will finish it, further it, and execute it.

A lot of people believe in positive affirmations, but remember that an affirmation without discipline and action is a delusion!

"You may encounter many defeats, but you must not be defeated" **Maya Angelou**

Persistence

"You need to recognize and sweep aside certain weaknesses which stand between you and your goals. Your persistence devel- ops into a respected, proved, progressive power." Napolean Hill

Woman on the Move

One Sunday afternoon after brunch with the family I was watching a special ***"I Have a Dream"*** Documentary. They were highlighting several remarkable stories of achievement and one particular story really stood out to me. It was about an African American Woman who was an aspiring entrepreneur. She worked for many years at different radio stations and thought about one day owning a radio station. When she decided to make the shift, to her realization it was no easy task. Once bold enough she started the process to- wards ownership and needed $1.2 Million dollars to acquire her first station. She embarked on a journey to convince banks and funders to lend her $1.2 Million even though she worked at radio stations but had no experience as a business owner of radio sta- tions. She was gracefully turned down after 33 presentations to access financial resources and because of persistence and belief pre- sentation 34 was her meal ticket. A Hispanic woman who had faith in her and felt her passion for what she wanted took a chance when other bankers said no business experience, no way. Whether it was good fortune or the personal feminine connection they made, fund- ing was secured for her first radio station. Every dime went into the stations acquisition and marketing. She had no money to do anything else including living expenses so for the first 18 months of her new business she slept on the floor of the radio station in a sleeping bag. Imagine that, waking up and washing up in the bathroom of her new company and when the doors opened, it was game time. Being an entrepreneur takes a different way of thinking and being. You must be willing to be called crazy at times as long as you believe in what you are striving for. There is an old adage that still holds true that says "You must be willing to do today what others are not willing to do, to have tomorrow what others will not have". No matter how big or small your dream is, others will not see it, which is why it was given to you and not them. The woman mentioned went on to build one of the largest portfolios of radio stations and is now labeled a media mogul, worth millions of dollars. When you're clear about what you and attached to that is a plan of action along with persistence for the roadblocks the possibilities are endless. Do you complain about your bed and justify being grouchy every-day? What if you slept on the floor for almost 2 years like the woman in the passage, could you face each day with optimism and hope to build a multi-million dollar business? Something to think about if you desire success, which is not automatic because as Gods children we deserve and have the right to success but it's up to us.

"Just what makes that little old ant think he can move that rubber tree plant?" <u>Sammy Kahn</u>

In being persistent there will be red flags along the journey that something is not working. Persistence does not mean repeating the same mistakes over and over again and subjecting yourself to a never ending cycle of pain.

Purpose

"Choose your road with care, but always choose a destination first" <u>Joseph Alessio</u>

The moment you discover your purpose and verbally go into covenant with God is the moment adversity will magnify in your life, it's called *PREPARATION*.

"There are powers inside of you which, if you could discover and use, would make of you everything you ever dreamed or imag- ined you could become." <u>Orison Swett Marden</u>

In discovering your <u>Purpose</u> ask yourself these questions:

Are there some areas in my life that are broken?

Am I searching for mental freedom and peace of mind from circumstances that I just can't figure out?

Do I desire closure from past relationships, hurts, or family conflicts?

Are there societal issues that make my heart

ache? What issues keep me up at night?
The answers to these questions may contain some insight to your purpose.

Purpose will camaflouge itself under pain and adversity, trust me.

*"The successful person has the habit of doing the things failures
don't like to do. They don't like doing them either necessarily. But their disliking is subordinate to the strength of their pur- pose."* <u>E. M. Gray</u>

While in student mode I was listening to Jesse Duplantis and he said something profound in his message titled "Waste Not Want Not"

- Your blessings may be in your fragments.
- The fragments may seem insignificant, but they may possess the greatest breakthrough your life has ever seen.
- Learn to piece together the fragments and the whole may be a fortune.

"Pursuing your purpose will extend your life." <u>Les Brown</u>

"As you choose your path and began to chase your dreams it must be supported by *purpose* and *meaning*, if not you will run out of gas. Your motivation and drive can't be money or mate- rial possession then he said *"If you eat enough lobster it begins to taste like soap"*. <u>Dave Ramsey</u>

Chapter Reflections

List 3 Things about your Perspective that has changed as it relates to the P-Diamond.

How will you use it to better your life and the lives of others?

Drive Destiny Depth
Determination Distinction

Chapter V
D-diamond

Determination – a firm resolve or intention. The quality of being firmly resolute. The fixing of the size, quality, amount etc. of any- thing; also, the result of this.

Drive – to propel onward or forward. A journey in a vehicle. Ener- gy; vitality. An organized campaign to achieve a certain goal.

Depth – The state or quality of being deep. Extent or distance. The innermost part; the part of greatest intensity.

Distinction- A distinguishing mark or quality; a characteristic dif- ference. Fame; eminent reputation. Excellence; superiority. A mark of honor.

Destiny- That to which any person or thing is destined. Inevitable necessity; fate.

The D Diamond truly gets to the core of who you are. It's the fuel to the force and intensity of your natural self. As I dive into it lets look at the D Diamond and connect it to your per- sonal brand. Most times when you here brand you think of a product or a company that sells a product.

Determination

Mark Zuckerberg/Facebook

When you are determined to accomplish a goal, no matter how big or small have a no quit attitude. This doesn't mean you should ignore obvious evidence that you are going down the wrong road. I call it blind determination. You must first be clear that you put de- termination towards something you truly desire and have a person- al connection to. Be aware that desire alone must also partner with ability. With ability and some skill level now accuracy, efficiency and effectiveness will come over time if you are determined. As my example I'll use Mark Zuckerberg the founder of Facebook. (Add other facts) As Facebook began to rise in popularity and add millions to its user base, here comes the larger companies look- ing to buy Facebook from Zuckerberg. First Yahoo offers him $1 Billion Dollars to buy him out and then MTV offers him $1.5 Billion and to many people's amazement he turns them both down. Remember that he has a team of people that was with him from the very beginning of Facebook's development. Because he had a clear understanding of what he envisioned for the Facebook name and brand he did not dismiss that vision for the highest bidder. Imagine the conversations at the Facebook office amongst the people who helped grow the Brand. I'm sure different sentiment was floating around but I believe those individuals also understood the vision and its greater potential if it remained in the right hands.

Depth

Proverbs 19;8

"He who gets wisdom loves his own soul; he who cherishes un- der- standing prospers"

You often hear people say wow that was deep if someone says something profound or quote a famous person but saying some- thing deep and being a person of depth is extremely different. A person with a good memory can quote the right things or remem- ber poems and quotes that someone wrote. It takes a different set of beliefs to become a person of depth and not only one who gets excited about superficial aspirations, instant gratification and self- ish motives. Depth is a way of life and not a rehearsed moment. To live a life of depth is not hard once you make the decision to live in your purpose everyday! A few paradigm shifts must take place for this to happen. One area is your personal philosophy about life and what determines a quality of life. ***Abundance vs. Survival***

Which of these mentalities best describe you?

Acts 5:12

"All the believers were one in heart and mind. No one claimed that any of his possessions was his own, but they shared everything they had. With great power the apostles continued to testify to the
resurrection of the Lord Jesus, and much Grace was upon them all. There were no needy persons among them. For from time to time those who owned lands and houses sold them, brought the money from the sales and put it at the apostle's feet, and it was distributed to anyone as he had need.

Someone with the ***abundance*** mentality can live a drastically dif- ferent life than someone with the ***survival*** mentality.

Abundance Mentality

- **Above average**
- **Takes constant work**
- **More than enough**

- Delayed Gratification
- Creates Win-Win Situations
- Deposits into others
- Lifetime learner
- Always Operates with Integrity
-

Above Average

This mentality is found in someone who strives for excellence and is not satisfied with being average. They practice longer, get up earlier and are never content with yesterday's victory.

Takes constant work

Always developing and refining your skill. Work on your craft even when you are called the best or one of the best. Always open to wise counsel. Bragging does not exist.

More than enough

You have a mentality and knowledge of life's abundance and therefore have no reason to be selfish, hateful or arrogant towards others. You don't think there is a lack of and so you are willing to share resource and ideas.

Delayed Gratification

You are willing to wait for certain things. Never pretending to be more than you are or having more than you have to impress others. You will give before you receive.

Creates win-win situations

Whenever you interact with others always create situations where all parties involved are put in a better situation. If you win and others lose you just broke the chain of destiny.

Deposits into other

They have a heart for people and will sometimes sacrifice themselves to help others win. Believes in empowering those they have access to never insulting them. Become intentional with your influ- ence and not with expectations of getting something.

Lifelong learner

Become 90% student and 10% teacher. Spend most of your time learning and broadening your perspective. Never *arrive* at great- ness even when others give you that label. Live the rest of your life passionately pursuing *Greatness! Always operates with integrity*

Integrity is doing the right because it's the right thing. Being hon- est and truthful when no one is looking allows you to sleep well at night. Make sure this is a part your life's core values and if you start a business, make it a part of your company's core values.

Survival Mentality

- **Not enough**
- **Average**
- **Selfish motives**
- **Instant Gratification**
- **Withdraws from others**
- **I know enough to win**
- **Do whatever it takes/Situational ethics**

Not Enough

There is a belief that there is a limit on resources and/or money and they must acquire as much for themselves as possible. They have an attitude that permeates deception and dishonesty. I have to get mines by any means then worry about you.

Average

Being okay with mediocre or average results is not an ideal place to be. When my children say things like, it's a C but it's a passing grade, I don't except that. If you worked extremely hard and did your absolute best it's okay. I just can't accept you settling because it's a passing grade and now you do just enough to get a C when you have the potential to get a higher grade. As adults please strive for excellence in all that you do.

Selfish Motives

It's all about me is the dominant attitude. They could care less if you achieve your goals. They will sacrifice anybody to make themselves look good. Don't be surprise that they are not helpful to others. They want and need to get all the credit.

Instant Gratification

They must have it right now so whoever has to get left out doesn't matter. They would rather look blessed rather than be blessed.
They value material things over substance and relationships.

Withdraws from Others

They are always either criticizing or finding fault in others. People hate to see them coming because they are insulting in their con- versations. They come to you as a dump site for their problem but can't be found when you need someone.

I know enough to Win

When someone is at the height of their game and they feel like they have no more to learn is dangerous.

Do Whatever it Takes/ Situational Ethics

The goal is to win or get the desired result and not be ethical or honest in doing it. Whatever it takes to meet the budget or acquire the new contract or client is key, not stating facts and reporting honest numbers. Only do what's right when there are witnesses.

I challenge you to put time and energy into developing the Abun- dance Mentality. That is where the WINNER'S Re- side! If you struggle in any area of the Survival Mentality make a commit- ment to work on improving everyday while you verbally claim the Abundance Mentality!

Drive

To truly understand drive is to understand that it is less about the actions you take and more about what drives you, the motive, the why, the reason, the inner hunger that no one sees!

"Being professional is doing what you love to do even though you don't feel like doing it" Julius Ervin

"Wrong actions will not bury you, but wrong reactions will." John Maxwell

Distinction

What sets you apart from others in all areas of your life? In rela- tionships, community, career, business when your name is men- tioned by someone, what follows? Are you like everyone else or do you possess a unique personality? When you enter a room does the energy change in a positive way or a nega- tive way? What do your kids say about you when you're not around, are you celebrated or tolerated? What is the sentiment of your co-workers when you are out for an extended period of time? Do they wish you were back or do they quietly rejoice in your absence?

These are the questions that most of us do not ask because we are afraid of the truth. Even when we act like the opinions of others don't matter deep down inside we do care how others see us. These questions are simply to assist us in developing the right attitude, personality and reliability that give us distinction and magnetic appeal to others.

"Good can be the enemy of the best" Joel Osteen

6 Characteristics of a Quality Brand (YOU)

- **Consistent**
- **High Integrity**
- **Able to Add Value/ Create Value- this exponentially increases earning potential**
- **Instant Recognition**
- **Trustworthy**
- **Comfortable (customers, co-workers, partners, vendors, family members)**

James 3:13

"Who is among you who is wise and intelligent? Then let him by his noble living show forth his good works with the unobtrusive humility which is the proper attribute of true wisdom."

"Man has no nobler function than to defend the truth." Ruth McKinney

Distinction is simply what separates you from everyone else. This is true in all areas of your life from home to the office to your community. To stand out from the crowd is not very hard to do in today's society. On most jobs the average person does just enough to not get fired and will get paid just enough to not quit. Both par- ties are being cheated because the company never gets the benefit of your additional skills or the going the extra mile work ethic you possess, while you're only compensated based on the value your resume outline. A few tips for the job to become a man or woman of distinction. Come in early and stay late, come up with ideas to improve efficiency and think of ways to help the company save money. These are just a few but they work and- you will come under workplace scrutiny- so what, you are after distinction not popularity in the average/conformity club. Even the way you treat people by being kind and courteous will make you stand out. When you become a person of distinction the world of opportunity will open up for you and you will become an enemy to mediocrity and those who've bought into & settled for mediocrity.

In your quest to become a man or woman of Distinction keep the following points in mind:

- Don't keep score when you go above and beyond for others.

- Never withhold helpful information if you can't use it yet and someone else can.

- If your day is not going well others should never become your punching bag so find other healthy alternatives for releasing your tension.

- Be proud and grateful for where you are and NEVER pretend that you have more than you do or can do something that you can't. Success takes time.
- Never destroy someone's character to build up your own. Be the example of distinction and quality.
- Celebrate along the journey because there will be many destinations.
- Become known for creating WIN-WIN situations

Adopt what I call THE RE-DEFINITION Attitude
RE-DEFINITION- is when you redefine negative sit- uations and circumstances that occur in your life and replace it with a meaning that's in line with where you're going in your life.

Here are a few examples:

1. *Problems become Possibilities*
2. *Difficulties become Character Building Moments*
3. *Adversity becomes Authority*
4. *Pain becomes Power*
5. *Negative People become Motivators*
6. *Set-backs become Set-ups*
7. *No's become Fuel*

This is key because these times can reveal emotional flaws that can ruin what you've become, especially on the journey towards distinction. This process is not an easy task because it will come with certain emotions that normally cause us to react, which then justifies the decisions we make, positive or negative. My hope is that we re-define these moments so that we respond accordingly and maintain our distinction. In the times that you loose control because we are human, you must love yourself through the process and continue striving for improvement.

Destiny

Where am I going and how fast do I want to get there?

Is destiny more about a particular destination some- where in the future or about our daily disciplines and activity that leads us in the direction of our destiny?

Ecclesiastes 9:11/12

"I have seen something else under the sun: The race is not to the swift or the battle to the strong, nor does food come to the wise or wealth to the brilliant, or favor to the learned; but time and chance happen to them all.

Moreover, no man knows when his hour will come:

As fish are caught in a cruel net, or birds are taken in a snare, so men are trapped by evil times that fall unexpect- edly upon them. ***"There are powers inside of you which, if you could discover and use, would make of you everything you ever dreamed or imagined you could become."***

Orison Swett Mardin

Chapter Reflections

List 3 Things about your Perspective that has changed as it re- lates to the D-Diamond.

How will you use it to better your life and the lives of others?

Soldier Significance Saint
Scholar Society

Chapter VI
S-Diamond
(Specific for Men)

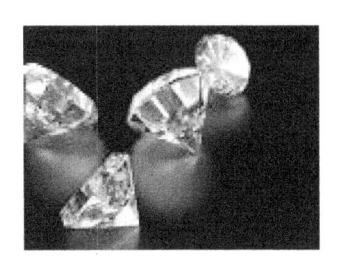

S Diamond for Men
(Extremely beneficial for women also)

Saint- A holy or sanctified person. A member of any of certain reli- gious sects calling themselves saints. A very patient, unselfish person.

Soldier- A person serving in an army. A brave, skillful, or experi- enced warrior. One who serves a cause loyally.

Scholar- A person eminent for learning. An authority or spe- cial- ist in an academic discipline. One who learns under a teacher. A pupil.

Society- A group of people, usu *Destiny*- That to which any per- son or thing is destined. Inevitable necessity; fate.

Significance- Importance; consequence. That which is signified or intended to be expressed; meaning

2nd Timothy 3:16

"All scripture is God-Breathed and is useful for teaching, cor- rect- ing and training in righteousness, so that the man of God may be thoroughly equipped for every good work.

The Proper Context

Although the S-Diamond was written for men that does not exclude its importance for women. The content will help women understand more about their male counterpart and how to Love them without taking certain things personal or feeling like they don't understand because sometimes we don't. We are wired differ- ent and the view point of men may differ not because we are being difficult but more because of genetics. I watch couples fight to get each other to be more like one another and that will not happen. It may take some paradigm shifts to get to this point of understanding but here is something to try the next time you and your spouse or mate get into a dispute. Try to view the dispute from their perspec- tive. Remember that our perspective is sometimes shaped by our experiences past and present which is totally different from person to person. You may find out that both parties are absolutely right coming from their perspective but because each person argues to be more right than the other they never validate the other's point on the matter. I have been happily married for 17 years and early on I struggled with certain view- points that my wife had until it
hit me. One example is how my wife responds when she hears about any type of storm that is on the horizon and coming our way. Her first thought is to get groceries in the house, have plenty of water and other supplies, i.e. flashlights and candles. That is way too much preparation, was how I initially thought until we had
a heartbreaking conversation about a storm that her family en- countered back home in Belize. A tropical storm hit their city and not only did property damage happen but her grandfather lost his wife and seven children and to make matters worse he could hear them call out to him while they perished in the water. With tears in my eyes I write these lines because this was an aha moment in my relationship and a new appreciation for my wife who endured
childhood pain that I would never know or feel. That pain fuels her response so we no longer argue about what we need during a storm because I validate and respect her perspective.

Why do you think break-ups happen so fast and easy? Minor disputes act like a virus and permeate the entire relationship because neither party would compromise and validate the other. The staggering result is 50 % of marriages ending in divorce.

There are lots of single women raising sons that will change as they age and unlike raising daughters they will be different and at times seem like there really from another planet. I have an eight year old daughter and certain issues are directed to my wife and with my sons certain issues are directed to me. While that gives us a beautiful balance it is not everyone's reality. It will be important for women raising sons to make sure he is exposed to positive, productive, hard working men because they will search for male affirmation at any cost. Young men will yearn for affirmation and acceptance which is why some lean towards negative behavior and/ or gang activity even with a hard working, church going mother.

This is not absolute for boys more so than girls because girls will also seek male affirmation sometimes becoming vulnerable for male violation. In a typical situation the first man that a girl will love is her father and if he is absent from the equation she may seek an unhealthy form of that love. An unhealthy relationship with a father who is present will strongly affect her relationship with her male counterpart as well. So it is extremely important to have positive and trustworthy male role models around your sons and daughters if their father is not in the picture to reinforce that strong male influence. This does not minimize the many aspects that mothers give to their children but it's extremely important.

Job 7:17-18

"What is man… that You should visit him every morning, and test him every moment?"

Psalms 45; 1-4

"My heart is stirred by a noble theme as I recite my verses for

the king; my tongue is the pen of a skillful writer. You are the most ex- cellent of men and your lips have been anointed with grace, since God has blessed you forever. Gird your sword upon your side, O mighty one; clothe yourself with splendor and majesty. In your majesty ride forth victoriously in behalf of truth, humility and righ- teousness; let your hand display awesome deeds. Let your sharp arrows pierce the hearts of the King's enemies; let the nations fall beneath your feet.

Significance:

Note: Significance is a choice, it's not your destiny.

Every man has a KING and a FOOL in him. The one you feed will thrive. Which one are you feeding? Which one are you al- lowing others to feed?

Characteristics of Both:

KING

- *Driven by Honor*
- *Influence*
- *Power*
- *Decisive*
- *Access to Resources*
- *Responsible*
- *Able to delegate*
- *Attention to detail*
- *Protective & Protected*
- *Motivated by a Challenge*
- *For the People*

FOOL

- *Driven by Pride*
- *Immature*
- *Procrastinator*
- *Manipulative*
- *Easily influenced*
- *No Verbal Filter*
- *Deceitful*
- *Unaware*
- *Unprotected*
- *Easily Defeated*
- *Selfish*

Psalms 45;16/17

"Your sons will take the place of your fathers; you will make them princes throughout the land. I will perpetuate your memory through all generations; therefore the nations will praise you for- ever and ever."

A person of significance gets people to look at things from the lens of curiosity as opposed to the lens of criticism and judgment. A person of significance operates with vision and not sight alone. ***"Isn't sight and vision the same thing"***, not at all? Sight is what you see with the natural eye, while vision is more of your mind's eye, or the mental picture of what you will become or accomplish. Take two individuals one is blind and the other is not. The person who can see has no direction for their life, no dreams, no goals, no aspirations, just existing and going through the motions of life. The blind person is currently taking college courses at a school for the blind. The blind person also has aspirations of becoming a world renowned writer and published author. The person who could see had no vision for their life, while the person who could not see had great vision for their life.

Add more content to the aforementioned

Reference Jawanza Kunjufu's Book "Keeping Black Boys out of Special Education"

- Special Education in America is now a $60 Billion dollar a year industry, so why mess with that much revenue! Someone is winning, it's not the kids pushed into Special Education when they are more than capable of learning and performing.

Began to see yourself as part of a perfect operating system/ ma- chine.

Entrapy- is when a part of a machine breaks down and eventu- ally breaks down the machine.

As a man you are called to be leaders of your homes, communities etc. You must be spiritually built up because the enemy will attack you first. When you cut off the head (Man) it will make the rest
of the body (Families, communities) weak, vulnerable and it will eventually die.

Parts of a man and what would happen if they break down

- **Brain**
- **Heart**
- **Lungs**
- **Kidneys**
- **Veins**

The man would eventually break down, causing the machine that he is a part of (his body) to break down.

That means the same is true when the man is out of place and broke down as it relates to the community and his family. Here are a few things that break down:

- The Family Unit
- Young men in the community
- Young women in the community
- Strong leaders (lack of)
- Relevant role models (lack of)

As men a lot of our anger comes from:

- Unreleased Tears ref. "When The Tears Won't Fall"
- Mis-Guided Fears

Un-Released Tears

As a boy growing up I would often hear the words "men don't cry", "toughen up and be a man", "don't let anyone punk you", don't be a mammas boy" and other statements that solidified what it meant to be a boy becoming a man. While I understand the root of these statements which often came from adult men in the family and community- I also understand the negative effects of these one sided statements. We were not taught how to process feelings be- cause they were suppressed and kept in. If someone did something offensive to you, a fight was the solution and if the offense was great enough many times fatalities were prevalent. If you suffered an emotional circumstance in your life and tears were justified but you were holding on to a belief that boys/ men don't cry this be- comes fertile ground for seeds of anger and frustration. Situations that lead to fights and other violent acts can almost always trace back to un-released tears along the way. When my mother passed away I shed tears, but I tried to sensor how much I cried until one day in the shower I lost it to the point where my wife had to come in the bathroom and ask if I was okay. As I reassured her that I was okay I got out of the shower and to my amazement I felt heaviness lifted that was on me since the day she passed. That day was an awakening in my spirit and I had a eureka/aha moment. The power of releasing tears was clearer than ever before. I thought of all the men who never allowed themselves the freedom of letting the tears flow. I thought of all the women who never got the best from their husbands because they were secretly angry. I thought of all the children who never knew the love of a deserving father because his father didn't love him and it was unfamiliar. Maybe this is the rea- son 50% of marriages end in divorce, I'm just saying. It was neces- sary to shed light on this because I observe this struggle in men all the time and I'm also guilty of starting fatherhood wrong 19 years ago. I too, said boys/men don't cry and all the other stuff as well.

Even today I find myself saying certain things as it relates to my two sons but I also give them the full spectrum of what I'm saying. I always let them know that there is a difference in whining about something that needs to be dealt with and pain, adversity and hurt from real life circumstances that may cause them to shed tears. As a mature husband and father it is emotionally healthy to cry when necessary. You don't lose man-points, trust me. You gain a greater respect from your loved ones, especially your sons and daughters. You also connect to the sensitivities of your wife and you think dif- ferently about the old adage that women are so emotional or more emotional than men. We are all emotional with different reference points and different triggers. Remember that there are a multitude of emotions that go with the human experience. While watching a movie one night I heard something that was relative to this point.

The wealthy businessman was speaking to his daughter about her husband, which was his son-in-law and they were trying

to figure out what was going on with him lately. The wife thought it was work and the father thought it was home that was troubling him. The wife then asked about a past near tragedy that happened and then said it can't be that because he never talks about it. The father then said *"The things that men don't talk about can be tearing them up inside and can ultimately destroy them"*. Point being,
if you're a man reading this section please check the gauges and make sure there is no unresolved hurt or pain that is stifling your emotional maturity. For any women reading this section take note of what your husband or partner may be dealing with that may
be doing the same and if your raising sons remember that healthy emotions are necessary but allow him to be a strong boy and show the balance when its necessary to cry.

"A man's pride is the hardest thing to expose" Robert Griffen Jr.

Mis-Guided Fears

Every person walking the planet has a fear of something that they deal with. It may be a fear of something small like a spider or big like a dog or lion. I know my son hates spiders even more than his fear of dogs. One day while walking my daughter to school someone was walking with a pitbull and so I pulled my daughter a little closer to me. She said daddy I wasn't scared was you? At first I paused because at that very moment I was terrified. She said I noticed that you pulled me closer but you didn't switch sides with me, the side the dog was on. I said while laughing, "sweety your younger than me so you'll heal quicker than me if you get bit. We both laughed and she said "that's wrong daddy. I was chased by the identical looking pitbull a few years prior and I had a flash-back that morning. The other part of this story is her ability to be bold because I was walking beside her and she knew me. I was her FATHER and she knew that if that dog came her way I would do everything in my power to protect her. Ask yourself the question do your family feel safe with you. Does your community see as a difference maker and a leader? What fears have you not dealt with that keep you limited in your potential? The physical and external fears are easy to deal with, but what do you do when those secret, hidden fears rise up but nobody can see them but you. Men battle with self-esteem and phobias also. If you are a woman living with a man or raising a boy to become a man become aware of some of the challenges that men also face, even if you don't understand them totally.

It is easier to build strong children, than to repair broken men"
Frederick Douglas

"As Men we define ourselves by what we have" **Steve Harvey**

- Cars
- Power or the illusion of it
- Homes
- Material Possessions

Answer:

What is the problem with that?

- **It feeds an unhealthy ego**
- **Morality may be compromised to get them**
- **We replace significance with stuff**

Excellence in small things will lead to a life of significance

Proverbs 13;22

"A good man leaves an inheritance for his children's children"

In life you can't choose how long you will live, but you can choose how well you live.

Tupac Shakur Quote: *"YOU MAY SPARK THE BRAIN THAT CHANGE THE WORLD"*

What if all we did was spark brains every-day. Become intentional about it knowing this may be the brain that really does change the world, finds a cure for Aids or ends world hunger. This puts things that we take for granted in a different perspective, like being a big brother, a mentor, a coach, mother, pastor or manager. Those and other roles put us in a position to spark a brain. *"How do I spark a brain"?*

Phillipeans 1;6

"The same God that started this good work, is the same God that will finish it, further it, and execute it.

Deuteronomy 29;29

"The secret things belong to the Lord our God, but the things re- vealed belong to us and to our children forever, that we may follow all the words of this law.

Soldier, Scholar, Saint, Society

1ˢᵗ Samuel 16;18

"One of the servants answered "I have seen a son of Jesse of Beth- lehem who knows how to play the harp. He is a brave man and a warrior. He speaks well and is a fine looking man. And the Lord is with him."

Question: If you possessed these same qualities what impact would you have on society

Describe your four top characteristics and your base characteristic (Create Your Diamond)

1st Samuel 17;32-35

David said to Saul, "Let no one lose heart on account of this Phi-
listine; your servant will go and fight him."

Saul replied, "You are not able to go out against this Philistine and fight him; you are only a boy, and he has been a fighting man from his youth."

But David said to Saul, "Your servant has been keeping his father's sheep. When a lion or a bear came and carried off a sheep from the flock, I went after it, struck it and rescued the sheep from its mouth. When it turned on me, I seized it by its hair, struck it and killed it."

What did David have working for him? He was confident in his ability to defeat the Giant Philistine. He was skilled in the use of a slingshot.

Why was David so confident? *As a boy he was successful in de- feating and killing a lion and a bear. He had faith in the God that he served.*

When the WHY is big enough the HOW becomes irrelevant

Note: Look at the incentive bestowed on the man who could defeat the Philistine. **David's WHY was big enough before he became aware of the King's incentive.**

1st Samuel 17;25

"Now the Israelites had been saying, "Do you see how this man keeps coming out? He comes out to defy Israel. **The King will give great wealth to the man who kills him. He**

will also give his daughter in marriage and will exempt his family from taxes in Israel."

Imagine going into this as a boy who tends to the sheep, coming out financially set, the king's daughter for your wife and tax ex- emption for your family. David did defeat the Philistine and his family was blessed because of his bravery. He stepped out with faith, belief and confidence in the God he served and was reward- ed handsomely. Apply this to your life and ask yourself if you've lacked faith, belief and confidence in any area of your life, if so, what area. Make a decision to be bold and claim victory then go to war like David and defeat the obstacles one by one. You already possess everything you need to become the victor and not the vic- tim.

Soldier:

Proverbs 14;29

"A patient man has great understanding, but a quick tempered man displays folly."

Courage is not the absence of fear

Courage is the ability to go from failure to failure and not lose enthusiasm

Courage is maintaining your confidence even after a loss

Courage is facing defeat, dusting yourself off and saying "I'll be back"

"Life is a fight for territory" Les Brown Proverbs 20;29
"The glory of young men is their strength, gray hair the splen-

dor of the old"

As a **soldier** you must identify your biggest fear/s and face it/them. Make sure you have reason to be fearful of whatever it is. Get all the pertinent information and never have what's called **"Condi- tioned Responses"**, which is responding the way you always do or the way others respond with no evidence of its validity. How are we conditioned? Here is a partial list.

- Friends
- Family
- Co-workers
- The media
- Religion
- Political parties

Proverbs 20;3

"It is a man's honor to avoid strife, but every fool is quick to quar- rel."

Deuteronomy 20;1

"When you go to war against your enemies and see horses and chariots and an army greater than yours, do not be afraid of them, because the Lord your God, who brought you out of Egypt will be with you"

If you have never paid attention to the discipline of ants, it's remarkable. While they are small their strength is in the numbers, which allow them to have unbelievable preparation. They can thrive against larger insects because of preparation. As a soldier sometimes you're outnumbered and in unfamiliar territory. What do you do during these times?

- First, face the reality that you are in a battle/war
- Before battle build strategic alliances
- Develop proper retreat or exit strategy
- Destroy the center of influence (person or information)

Point 1: Face the reality that you are in a battle Many times the battles we face are not physical. *Point 2:* Before battle build strategic alliances *Proverbs 20;18*
"Make plans by seeking advice, if you wage war, obtain guidance."

Point 3: Develop proper retreat or exit strategy *Point 4:* Destroy the center of influence *Deuteronomy 20;19*
"When you lay siege to a city for a long time, fighting against it to capture it, do not destroy its trees by putting an ax to them, because you can eat their fruit. Do not cut them down. Are the trees of the field people, that you should besiege them? However, you may cut down the trees that you know are not fruit trees and use them to build siege works until the city at war with you falls." **Or the situa- tion, crisis or obstacles in your life!**

Reference "Protect Your Soil"

Protecting implies that something is opposing, coming against, or threatening what you are protecting.

T*his also means that you are fighting to protect IT. Let's list what IT is:*

Tangible

- *Yourself*
- *Your Family*
- *Your Community*
- *Your Home*
- *Your Church*
- *Your City/State/Country*
-

Intangible

- *Your Mental Capacity*
- *Your Peace of Mind*
- *Your Joy & Happiness*
- *Your Emotional Stability*
- *Your Purpose*
- *Your Energy*
- *Your Time*
- *Your Faith*

Note: When we lose at protecting the intangible it lessens our chance to effectively protect the tangible

Stop and think for a moment of all of the safeguards that we put around the things in our lives that are tangible. We protect our- selves from weather conditions with clothing and shelter. Our community is protected by law enforcement, while our homes and businesses are protected by security systems. On the other hand, what protects the intangible, the internal things that make up our being? Most of us are not intentional about protecting these things because they are not visible. Once you decide to become more in- tentional about this you will begin to monitor what you read, who you hang around and what you do with your time and energy. This is the sacred part of the human experience but it remains exposed to any and everything because we don't protect it. We give up our peace of mind by working at jobs that give us no fulfillment and has very little growth. We spend time around people that drain our energy and complain about life instead of living their full potential. Sometimes life deals us a bad hand but often times you do have the power to choose your environment, friends and circumstances. I have witnessed folks initiate the circumstances, create an environ- ment of turmoil, include troublemakers and then add fuel to the fire when it begins to diminish. Your decisions can be a form of protec- tion just like a weapon. Your decisions can also act like the equivalent of a weak immune system without protection. It's your choice!

Soldier's Result

Deuteronomy 11;22-25

"If you carefully observe all these commands I am giving you to follow---to Love the Lord your God, to walk in all his ways and to hold fast to him---then the Lord will drive out all these nations before you, and you will dispossess nations larger and stronger than you. Every place where you set your foot will be yours: Your territory will extend from the desert to Lebanon, and from the Euphrates River to the Western Sea. No man will be able to stand against you.

Saint:

Saint in not a synonym for perfection

Job 1:8

"Have you consider My servant Job, that there is none like him on earth, a blameless and upright man, one who fears God and shuns evil?"

Disclaimer: It's more of a detriment when you're so spiritual that
you are no earthly good

There are many people who pray & tithe, sing and believe but nev- er build wealth and will speak against it as if it is outside of Gods order. I once heard Joyce Meyer say that **"Billions of dollars are being spent on experts trying to figure out what's wrong with humanity. "The Absence of God Is What's Missing."**

Spiritual Warfare should not be used as an excuse for our own lack of discipline and accountability

"The Devil Made Me Do It" has become the fallback for people who go to church and for those that do not go to church. This totally removes personal responsibility and gives people an easy out. While there are attacks that happen in our life that we have no control over we must also acknowledge when we are in control and must simply accept responsibility.

Proverbs 22;1

"A good name is more desirable than great riches: to be esteemed is better than silver or gold"

As we know every one of us has to check out one day. When they're reading your eulogy to the church they will never mention how big your house was or how many luxury cars you had. People could care less about the number of tailored suits you owned or how many exotic vacations you went on. What did the dash rep- resent? The dash between your born date and the date you passed away. People are there to remember and hear about how you treat- ed people and loved those close to you. What contributions you made to society. There is a quote that I came across many years ago that says it all *"Your character is the only thing that will walk back from the grave into the hearts of the people who knew him"*.

Proverbs 12;2

"A good man obtains favor from the Lord"

Results of being a Saint

Deutoronomy 11;13-15

"So if you faithfully obey the commands I am giving you today---to Love the Lord your God and to serve him with all your heart and soul---then I will send rain on your land in its season, both autumn and spring rains, so that you may gather in your grain, new wine and oil. I will provide grass in the fields for your cattle, and you will eat and be satisfied.

Line from

"You must close your eyes to open your soul" **Ludacris (Hip- Hop Artist)**

"Don't let anyone break your spirit to fuel their own confidence"..!

Society:

Question to Ponder: Do you know the difference between a CAST SOCIETY and the current society that you are a part of?

A Cast Society says that whatever you are born into you must be for the rest of your life. So if you are born a peasant or a slave you are supposed to die as a peasant or as a slave. You are to only socialize with and befriend others that are of your socio-econom- ic standing. I was watching a documentary about certain parts of India where the women were born into prostitution. I heard peo- ple speak about the cast system in India but I never had any real knowledge about the depth of a cast system until I watched this entire documentary. My heart was extremely heavy because I am the father of a precious eight year old daughter. I call her my little princess and was amazed to see fathers not only force or sell their daughters into prostitution, but also live off the earnings. If all of the women in the family were prostitutes then that was the fate of any daughter born into that family because of the culture of a cast system. Innocent girls as young as 9 or 10 years old were recruit- ed, forced and sold into a life of despair and abuse all because of where they were born.

As harsh as the realities of a Cast System are, many people who are not bound by this type of system function like they are. If you take a real hard look at the broader society, you will notice that most people are going through the motions of life and not living up to their full capabilities. Even in a free enterprise and capital- ist society folks who are born into low-income or impoverished conditions adopt that as their lot or final destination. Unlike a Cast System, you do have a choice as well as examples of how to break the cycle of poverty and create a better future than that of previous generations.

Proverbs 22;29

"Do you see a man skilled in his work? He will serve before kings; He will not serve before obscure men."

What is your role

What is our individual impact on society?

Have you committed a crime on society? Should you be convicted? By not becoming the greatest and most successful YOU possible, whose life is held hostage due to lack of achievement by you.

Most of us would say NO because we are not accustomed to look- ing at the things that are intangible, like desire, passion and com- mitment. In fact these are the characteristics that lead us toward achievement.

Here is the perspective I want you to look at it from. If you have children and they never see you becoming your best, what does that tell them? Their belief in themselves is partly influenced by your belief in them, but also by your belief in you. Children will always pay more attention to what you do and not what you say. If they see circumstances get the best of you it will impact how they respond to life's circumstances. The same will apply to your spouse and others that you have any type of influence over. You can spark dreams and instill hope in others with your own journey
towards success. This simply means that society needs your talent, ability and accomplishments to thrive. See yourself as a relevant participant and not as a curious observer. Would you like to know how to become aware of what it would take to be more of an ex- ample? Lets stop the crime of inactivity. Here's how!

Ask these questions of yourself:

- *Could I do better?*
- *Should I do better?*
- *Who's watching me?*

- *Does it matter?*
- *Do I matter, if so to whom?*

Proverbs 27:23

"Be sure you know the condition of your flocks, give careful atten- tion to your herds; for riches do not endure forever, and a crown is not secure for all generations"

The average individual measures themselves based on *societies* expression of beauty, success and fame and most times fixing the external parts become the focal point.

- Body,
- Attire,
- Face,
- Weight,
- Material Possessions.

You hear statements like I would be happy with a perfect body, had a better car, lost this weight, had more money in the bank or had
a better spouse. True development and personal enhancement can only happen from the inside out, not the outside in. The goal of this entire project is to connect you to the internal you.

- Mind
- Heart
- Soul/Spirit

Working on the internal will allow you to accomplish any external success you desire. You will have the impact on *society* you desire. Control will remain in your hands no matter what the circumstanc- es are. *Society* will look to you for answers and solutions. You will be the example of success and not the case study for failure.

Proverbs 19;4

"Wealth brings many friends, but a poor man's friend deserts him"

Scholar:

Years ago I read a quote that said *"you never know the true reach*

or influence of a teacher"

"Thousands of geniuses live and die undiscovered either by

themselves or by others". Mark Twain

Information costs, but it pays for

itself *Proverbs 8;6*
"Listen, for I have worthy things to say; I open my lips to speak what is right."

Once you're labeled a scholar your awareness expands. Your impact will flow to others and expand their awareness and impact if that's their desire. Your results in life will always be an expres- sion of your awareness. Exponential growth happens when mul- tiple minds are impacted by scholars, teachers, philosophers, etc. Scholars also shape people's perspective and view of the world. I encourage those of you who have been labeled a scholar, teacher or educator to also remain a student to better your craft and to keep humility present at all times. I have witnessed folks who are la- beled scholars or intellectuals belittle others because of the dispar- ity in the information. I'll share an example of the danger of being the standard because of your title. If through your instruction,
educating or counseling your students feel like you are the standard and if they fall short of being just like you they are a failure, you must work to correct that. The power of influence

is in the hand of the influencer, while the influenced must still make the final deci- sion for their life. The goal is always to show a mentee or student how to emulate the principles, habits and disciplines that brought you success but not to become YOU! The ideal reward is always when your influence helped someone discover their own ability and potential.

Proverbs 28;2

"When a country is rebellious, it has many rulers, but a man of understanding and knowledge maintains order."

Proverbs 13;14

"The teaching of the wise is a fountain"

Proverbs 14;8

"The wisdom of the prudent is to give thought to their ways"

Einstein Quote: *"The thinking that has brought me this far have created some problems that this thinking can't solve" "Where are my thoughts taking me" Jim Rohn*

***"Doing less than you can messes with the mind" Jim Rohn* Ecclesiastes 8;1**

"Who is like the wise? Who knows the explanation of things? Wis- dom brightens a man's face and changes its hard appear- ance."

Proverbs 20;15

"Gold there is and rubies in abundance, but lips that speak knowl- edge are a rare jewel.

A superior man is modest in his speech, but exceeds in his ac- tions" Confusious

This section was referenced in **Learn** *section of The L-Diamond*

We must always strengthen this part of our brain to remain intel- lectually productive.

Pre-Frontal Cortex is the executive part of the brain that gives you the ability to have:

- Forethought
- Judgment
- Organization
- Planning

We must become aware of all of the mental faculties of the brain to become better in every area of our lives, they are:

- ✓ Perception
- ✓ Will
- ✓ Memory
- ✓ Imagination
- ✓ Reason
- ✓ Intuition

"In the end, you can only teach the things that you are". Max Lerner

Chapter Reflections

List 3 Things about your Perspective that has changed as it re- lates to the S-Diamond.

_____
___ _____
_____
_____
___ _____
_____
_____
___ _____
_____

How will you use it to better your life and the lives of others?

_____
___ _____
_____
_____
___ _____
_____
_____
___ _____
_____

Destiny Foundation Life
Significance Purpose

The Diamond Project | By: Eric D. Hall

Chapter VII
LET'S START DIGGING
How It All Works

This final chapter is to help you identify some diamonds that already exist in your life in different areas. Once discovered you can be more intentional about when and how you bring out there true value.

A few thoughts to ponder:

- 1 hour per day reading and learning in your particular industry will make you an expert and add tremendous value to you.

- Don't put yourself in a container/jug that will limit your growth and potential.

- Look at your work like a person stand- ing off in the distance would and see the hid- den treasures in your current work or business. What are you missing?

- Have you developed your people skills to the point where you are a magnet for the right people and/or opportunities?

- Be intentional about growth then watch and measure the results.

- It's a lot of fun when you cross things off of your goals list.

LET'S START DIGGING

The Diamonds In You!

Who are you and why would there be diamonds in you? Even if you can't afford real diamonds at this present time that has nothing to do with the internal treasures and untapped wealth you carry around every-day. Once you realize the treasures in *YOU* and then develop a proper strategy for utilizing them in your life, that's when your life will be whatever you decide it will be. You can make as much money as you desire. You can work in the industry of your choice. You can have the quality relationships that enrich you. You can travel if you want. You can fight the injustices that bother you. You can organize and attack education reform or hun- ger. You can contribute to causes that you are passionate about and so much more. Okay let's simplify the big picture stuff and make it plain and practical. Let's develop a process for you based on where you are right now. The things you need to work on will take time especially if they are habits that have been present for many years. Habits are as powerful as an addiction to drugs so the task of breaking old and /or bad habits can be daunting without con- sistent new habit replacement. You must work as hard as possible to discover what your purpose is because without knowing your purpose you will ultimately give up or throw in the towel when it
gets hard or uncomfortable. Something as simple as starting to read books on personal development and success will seem like a huge task if you get the biggest book on the shelf or attempt to read for 2 hours every night. Keep in mind that developing the new habit
is the key and not the amount of time or quantity. If it feels like a task or an undesirable job it will take no time at all to quit the new habit. Read something positive and encouraging for 10 minutes a day or commit to 1 or 2 pages. Trust and believe the way the mind works is simple and once new infor-

mation enters- it will desire more, especially if you see results from the information. A popular adage says that *"a man's mind once it expands it never returns to its original dimensions"*. Once the mind expands a new awareness will show up and you no longer rely on everyone else for insight but you start to trust yourself and gain confidence in your ideas.
Then action will replace procrastination. *Now,* the importance of skill development is realized by you and the cycle continues. As you enhance your skills and abilities and become more efficient and results are consistent, next step is to seek mentorship from those well accomplished in your area of interest and allow them to cut time off of your learning curve. This pattern can be used for any new venture, job or project you embark upon. Develop this
process as a way of life and not just to achieve a few goals and you will continuously discover diamonds within you.

The Diamonds In Your Family!

<u>F</u>ocus <u>A</u>nything <u>M</u>ajor <u>I</u>n <u>L</u>oving <u>Y</u>ourself

While this section calls on your ability to recognize the Diamonds in your entire family, don't be guilty of missing the Diamonds in your household. Your spouse, your kids and the internal culture you establish as a family are rare and may offer value to other families. We have family game and movie night and those times solidify the bond and become a fun and positive outlet in a some- times negative world. You will find out what your spouse and kids are truly interested in. In your household there is no facade or pretending so being yourself is the norm. While every household is different and every member of the family is different it can be unique in the way that you learn and enjoy each other's gifts and
talents. Be careful as your children exhibit their gifts that you don't minimize their interest and encourage what you think they should be interested in. You may bury a diamond they are trying to find value in. As a parent it is not your job to choose but to encourage and provide the environment and the tools to

develop it. Something else to know is that it is equally dangerous to your kids and to humanity when you don't develop your diamonds and become all that you can be, as cliché as that sounds. Because I broke certain behaviors and tried the unfamiliar I was able accomplish a few things that hadn't been done in my family.

The Diamonds In Your Job!

Why do some people get promotions, enjoy work and make ad- vancement look so easy? They make it look like they have a special advantage or know something you don't know! They have learned to find the diamonds in their work because they view the job as more than just a job. The assumption is that a job pays you per hour when in reality they pay you for the *VALUE* that you put in that hour. If you are intentional about becoming more valuable to your employer the promotion you are seeking will be attainable. Whenever the company offers additional training become the first to take advantage of it and allow your resume to grow within the company. Access the college reimbursement program to getknowl- edge that will make you stand out and become a bigger asset to the company and not just your department. Develop intelligent objec- tivity about your specific job and others. That, is having the ability to look at your job from an outside perspective somewhat like a person wishing they had your job. When you are on the job it is sometimes hard to see how to become more valuable. With intel- ligent objectivity you see where the company can save money and become more efficient with small changes. Your mind will think more about innovation and less about the end of the work day. This is not always the case but when your name becomes synonymous with saving and making money, cutting costs and innovation, doors will open that are closed to those who simply show up for work.
Another way to find the diamonds in your work is to develop the ability to work with different types of people not just those you have things in common with. Develop a magnetic attitude and become good at working alone and/or with a team.

Develop dis- cernment in your spirit, become a great listener and avoid gossip, unless it edifies others. Understand how to delegate even if you're not a supervisor your team will count on it when doing projects and your name will create a buzz, *VALUE*!

The Diamonds In Your Business!

What business are you in? What products does your company offer? What means the most to you people or money when mak- ing important decisions about your business? Do you have clear core values for your company and do they permeate through every department or just your management team. This is relative even if you are a one man operation. Do you have a strategy to increase how many people you serve and how to broaden your impact?

Your business is an extension of you at first but as you add others to your vision make sure you have a system of personal develop- ment in place so that as your business and brand grows so does the perspective and skill of your team. When selecting your team

don't just review the resume of prospects but look for cultural fit and passion and excitement for what your company does and the industry you are in. When everyone is on the same page of a great vision people are more creative and willing to go the extra mile for the company's success. Have incentives for extra production
and results of your team. Allow people to flow in their gift with the necessary structure for daily results but growing your business will happen through innovation and ideas of the team.

The Diamonds In Your Community!

For this section I will speak about the neighborhood that made me the man I am today. As I personalize this section I trust that you will pick the gems out of the words and make it relative to your life and personal journey. I grew up in a neighborhood that is more recognized for the negative activity even with great things hap- pening at the same time. When I grew up I saw a lot of things that had an impression on my future. For awhile I played the victim until it dawned on me that I was in control of my life and not my surroundings. No matter what is happening in your neighborhood there are folks who get up everyday and strive to do good deeds and make a difference for others. You must find those circles of people and connect with them. You have great solutions to prob- lems that you think someone else will solve. Be bold and step out in faith and start your program to help the youth. Become a mentor to one person and grow it to more. Organize with others and start petitions to improve your community parks. Focus on solutions and become a creative problem solver. Whatever it takes to find the diamonds in your community, it starts with you.

The Diamonds In Books

"Education is the ability to meet life's situations" ***John G. Hibben***

Every great achievement was made by someone and then it was captured in a book. An autobiography or biography was written to illustrate their journey, mistakes and setbacks. Part of the fulfill- ment for widely successful individuals is to teach the principles and process that attained their notoriety. What greater feeling is there than to achieve greatness and then show others how to do it. When you purchase a book, you purchase someone's life, exper- tise and step by step how to information. Trimming time off of your learning curve can happen when a great book in your field helps you avoid the landmines that can otherwise set you back or subtract from your bank account. Develop the habit of reading by starting small with one page per day or a chapter a week. Read books that interest you and stir your curiosity. Reading has to be for more than entertainment so make sure you find personal devel- opment and how to books in your desired industry. Our brain needs exercise and stimulation as does the body so keep your mind fresh and sharp by feeding it good information and arousing all of its abilities. Books are the only way to a better life full of opportuni- ties and fulfillment. If you know some- one who can't read make it your business to change that and help them learn how. If someone can learn a new language then someone can learn to read.

"A man's mind once it's stretched never returns to its original dimensions"

"In order to get to the things on the higher shelf you have to stand on the books you read" **JimRohn**

The Diamonds In Others

Diamond in the Making By:
Alejandra's Story

How do you find your diamond? This seems like an easy question to answer, but the reality is that there's depth in it. Many people ask me, what motivated you and keep you motivated to continue strong into your healing journey through fitness? My response has always being emotional PAIN! What? I don't get it, Alejandra. Let me explain; when the pain is tangible that you can feel it through your veins, your heart expands and the heartbeat feels like an eruption is taking place in your chest. In that moment, when you want to pray for God to end your life, and then you recall you have kids that depend on you, that your parents will never be the same if they see you go before they do, and your siblings life would nev- er be the same, then you realized that being dead is not the right prayer. The real prayer is, thanks God for allowing this adversity into my life, because you have a plan for me. An unknown plan, but I will allow your mercy upon me, and will walk this journey with faith. Faith that the future is better than my past, faith that my present is the platform to build my future and that I can re-write the outcome, and that my past doesn't define me and it will not hold me hostage.

Please give me the strength to hold on the promise of something better, and allow me to walk through my pain to obtain real heal- ing. I must walk through to come out strong. I cannot walk around it, avoid it, or lock it in the closet. The healing process begins by feeling the pain and acknowledging the root causes. Then I began working on self-love and self-respect while the soul and my entire self felt demolished, worthless and unlovable. The bigger the pain, the harder I worked. It motivated me to push forward and not give up when I felt weak. The pain was so bad, I couldn't give up, I couldn't! Then one day I woke up and understood that God had a purpose for me "to be a voice for those that don't have a voice and to motivate others to claim themselves back from the shackles of abuse" and that was my turning point, I finally found my diamond, my true calling. Finally I took my power back from my abuser and I became a survivor rather than a victim. Find your calling, your diamond, change your mindset to freedom. I had to overcome obstacles and hardships to become a better person- that's true healing. I decided that the codependent and naive woman I once was needed to died so that a new woman can be reborn; a true Badass, a rough diamond in the making!

YaMo'ne Empowers By:
Kamilia Horsley

August 4, 2019 at approximately 7:30 am on a beautiful Sunday morning. I was listening to Mary Mary trying to motivate myself while driving to the gym. I saw this person stand in the street in front of a shinny black BMW. As I approached the person, I no- tice she was a pretty black girl with a yellow bikini top with black booty shorts and flip flops on. Her body language was intense and seductive and as I drove past, I thought to myself, why the hell is she standing in the middle of the street this early in the morning. After I got my workout on when I was traveling back, I saw that same young lady walking down the street with bags in her hands looking disheveled and defeated. In that very moment my heart started to hurt. I felt the pain that was on her face. See, ironically this young lady was me and I am her. I also struggled as a young lady and dealt with issues such as teen homelessness, teen domes- tic violence, teen pregnancy, drugs and std's. I was faced with the threat of death more than once at an early age. I know it's hard out here and then I thought to myself she needs a person like myself to tell her she can make it without selling her soul. I know because I did it! Baby girl you must know that the cards that you were dealt doesn't define who you are. What you

make of yourself is what shows the true character and testimony of a person's life. And that was just it! My DIAMOND! I asked God to show me how to use my gift and do it for a living. My DIAMOND is me and I am the DIAMOND! My life experiences and how I made it through is
my DIAMOND! After being raised with selfish drug addicts for parents and then put into the foster care system to getting sexually assaulted in foster care. I got the message from God that I am the product and the product is me. He has allowed me to empower and motivate others through hard times because I can relate to their struggles and pain. That is how YaMone Empowers was birthed.

YaMone Empowers is my brand and, is an umbrella of mind, body, soul and spirit healing services. I do motivational speaking engage- ments on various topics and provide other support services to help ones grow healthy, mentally, physically, spiritually and emotion- ally. God is allowing me to speak my truth to help others to find their DIAMOND! My story is authentic to me but very similar
to others at the same time. My faith is what pushed me to believe and to not give up and to die trying. This is no matter the circum- stances. So, despite all the time it took me to get ready for this very moment I would like to introduce myself: I am Kamilia YaMon'e Horsley aka Sweetk Horsley, a mother of three, CEO and owner of
YaMone Empowers, author and writer of my new upcoming book *13 Doors* " Abandoned by the System"! This is my story of how it all started and why I am still standing tall today! I want my story to help inspire others to push through to win in life and to turn their pain into success!!!!!!!!!!!!!

13 Doors "Abandoned by the System"!!!!
By Sweet K Horsley....

"Caged Bird"
By: Ms. Saskia Dasent

When I met Mr. Eric Hall, I was at a time in my life where I was broken and shattered. I was in a persistent depressive state with no way out. I felt like a caged bird just hoping for a day to somehow fly beyond my limitations. I was an undocumented immigrant from the Caribbean Island of Tortola. After my high school graduation, for 10yrs of no documentation, life stopped for me. All doors were shut, all opportunities were at a halt because of a number, I did not have. I went through a period of not knowing who I was. I suffered serious depression, but was great at masking such pain. The harder I laughed, the more I cried. I was spinning in a constant circle of darkness. Hiding in the shadows and fearing that somebody may expose my lack of identity. That nine digit number was the gate-way to life; it was like oxygen to the soul. How was I supposed to live if the very thing I needed was not available to me.

After being a student of life, and using life as my classroom, I set off on the personal development journey. Since I couldn't move around like the average person; in that interim, I just built my mind, constantly reading books to elevate my thinking. Even though society held me back, my mind was elevated to soar. I be- came a student of the LAW of ATTRACTION, speaking what you want into existence. Instead of being a victim of my circumstances, I started speaking things of faith.

Through prayer and developing the right perspective on life, I was granted my immigration status. The moment I shifted my mind on the things I could control, my circumstances started moving in my favor. My favorite quote, "Life is 10 percent of what happens to you, and 90 percent how you respond to it."

I found a passion in business ownership. I never viewed myself as a business owner, but to my surprise I was one of the few to hit an elite milestone in my company. Today I still continue to grow my business and service hundreds of customers on a monthly basis.

I've discovered the diamonds that I possess, which one is, help- ing people. There is no better feeling than to empower the people around you to do great things. Often times people are physically living but emotionally and spiritually dead. It takes diligence and intentionality to become the person you feel most proud of. I am currently working on a mantra to support and empower women around the world.

Mr. Eric Hall and the Hall Group have been truly instrumental in my growth and development. It has taught me that we all have dia- monds within us that we need to nourish and share with the world.

The Real Life Story of Donald Houston AKA Deke

Divine Intervention
By: Donald Houston (Deke)

The beginning is a story of bullying gone bad. Deke was 12 years old and he suffered at the hands of a bully that sort of took his child- hood. After this 16 year old teenager destroyed his Tonka Truck (Built to Last) then Deke stood up. The other kid gave Deke a beat- en that will become the motivation that would impact the rest of his natural life, good and bad. To add insult to injury his father coun- tered the bullies beating with a verbal beat down that could have sent him down an abyss of shame and embarrassment but instead a monster was born. Deke started lifting his older brother's weights to build strength and began to grow into the man, the boxer and the street legend. At age sixteen, Deke had a chance encounter with the childhood bully. Deke spots the bully crossing the street in Dudley Station but the bully had no idea of the years of shame that Deke experienced from that brutal beating that left Deke with both eyes closed and swollen, nose bloody, lip bust open, teeth missing and a broken Tonka Truck! He hit him so hard with the right hook that Deke stumbled from the second blow because the bully was on his way to the ground. Normally in life and boxing we may be motivated by competition and winning but Deke was taken back to a moment in time where he was hurt for no reason so he was motivat- ed by shame and guilt. **Because this kid was 16 at the time and beat Deke so bad for no reason, he would** catch a beat-down for the next 3 years every time Deke saw him. As he put on weight, muscle and strength he became the neighborhood look out for bullies. If you preyed on the weak he preyed on you. As he came to the aid of others he also began forming a team of followers that he taught what he knew. His first incident with crime was stealing money from a teacher. This evolved into a love for what others possessed, so he became a notorious stick-up kid. Deke would take drug dealers money, jewelry and drugs. Until a robbery happened that altered the course of the rest of his life. A certified hustler from Jamaica moving pounds of smoke (illegal marijuana) was the latest stick-up. Someone Deke had good business relations with until a crack was spotted in his armor. It was an opportunity for him to capitalize on this moment of vulnerability. This was no easy task because this guy was known for murder, mayhem and making lots of illegal money. His guard was down and Deke struck; the stick resulted in garbage bags of money and smoke. Shortly after, within a few hours, after dropping off smoke to different people and stash- ing the money Deke made his way back to Zeigler St. in OP. and was met with the words "Deke my man WHY YA GWAN HIT ME SPOT", he was then shot in the face and as he turned the next shot was to the back of his head. By now without falling to the ground he is reaching for his gun and gets shot a third time in the back. To everybody's amazement Deke never fell to the ground as he shot back and made it to a nearby hallway, bleeding like a running faucet. Thankfully and old friend was outside in his brand new Cadillac and drove Deke to the hospital. While in the hospital, after surgery and near death he gets indicted for old crimes he com- mitted. Motivated by shame and guilt no other thought plaqued his mind except for laying down every person who fired a shot at him. Once he was released from the hospital revenge and a new addic- tion accompanied him. The same painkillers the hospital introduced him too, started his use of different drug, primarily heroine. From this point in his life it was all downhill, shooting someone in the same spot he was shot on Zeigler St, now the indictment is served and he added attempted murder. It all resulted in a life sentence, *"he's a career criminal, throw-away the key"* they said. In prison he continued to sharpen his skills as a boxer and even trained inmates. While in prison his mother was murdered by his stepfather. During our interview Deke said when he lost his mother he lost his mind so every-day he would fight to take his pain out on his opponent. Again his motivation was shame and guilt. If I was out she would be alive because I would have killed him first before he killed my mother. During this time in prison 2 things kept him alive and that was boxing and the love of his mother. There was no time to show weakness or any other emotion that could easily turn you into a victim in prison. Trauma was a regular occurrence during his time witnessing everything from murder to suicide by hanging. Due to God's grace and divine intervention Deke was blessed to serve many years but nothing close to the life sentence he was given. Because of Divine Intervention you see how many situations he was able to make it through still alive and in his right state of mind mentally. He himself realized that only the grace of God kept him and in that grace was where he wanted to spend the rest of his life. Without the absence of struggle Deke made a commitment to God and boxing that would became a much needed asset in our community. Using training as an outlet he birthed a vision that was on his heart for many years; Houston Power Boxing, a Self Defense, Fitness and Boxing Training Program. Due to all the madness, mayhem and destruction that Deke brought to Boston and other cities he can never repay society or the people for his lost, traumatic and angry behavior. But by the Grace of God he is forgiven and he's living; as a husband, father, grandfather, coach and mentor too many. He is considered the People's Champ because of all the lives he has impacted over the past 20+ years. The bully and the Tonka Truck may have started it all, but God's Love and a Passion for Boxing and teaching along with more great community accomplishments will be the Legacy of Donald Houston (Deke)! *More to come in the Movie!*

Mission Hill to My Mission
By: Pastor Dallas

Pastor Everett Johnathon Dallas Jr. grew up in the housing devel- opment of Mission Hill. Pastor Dallas was exposed to a different lifestyle at an early age. In 2004 he was incarcerated for a period of time, it was not of his own wrong doings but it was the will and plan of God.

In June 2005 a new life began after his mother, Overseer Cassandra Dallas, reintroduced him to our Lord and Savior, Jesus Christ.

In the year of 2006 Pastor Dallas became a minister and the Na- tional Men's President within the Apostolic Faith. God began doing a quick work in his life. In February 2007 Pastor Dallas be- came an ordained Elder. In October of 2007 he was ordained as a Youth Pastor. In July of 2008 he was called to be the Youth Pastor and Assistant Pastor of "On A Mission True Holiness Church of the Apostolic Faith" under the leadership of his Pastor/mother Over- seer Cassandra Dallas.

Pastor Dallas was officially ordained Pastor of Living Word Church in April 2014. He stands for true holiness, and teaches and preaches to all to live a holy life. Pastor Dallas introduces people not to religion but rather to a relationship with Jesus

Christ. He is serious about holiness and his Lord and savior Jesus Christ.

Bullied from birth
By: Alethia Kindle

2nd grade hit and I started letting everyone who wanted it have it! No exceptions, respect was engraved in me. It was too late. Born into savagery. A vacation from life is exactly what we needed.
Pack up your stuff. Let's get to going, you'll suffer for miles with motion sickness and hours with regret. However, the regret really came when I realized I wasn't dreaming. I thought I was dream- ing. I just knew I had to be dreaming. Something like this could never happen to me. I could not be a victim. I could not be the typical girl. I opened my eyes and there his hands were under my shirt, beneath my bra. Gripping my barely developed chest as I fought. Because that one encounter I flew, I didn't agree with the feeling that defense mechanisms left me embodying. An uphill battle, already shifted in slope, downhill. Everything from there was downhill. I began fighting for everything I believed was rightfully mine. My name, my character, my respect, my appear- ance, my family...everything mine. The razors to my wrist weren't enough to suffice. The blood trickling, never felt like enough.
When it all came out years later through a mandated reporter, I couldn't help but feel I was to blame for all the turmoil that came next. *Ding dong* the bell rang and we all were confused. No one was expecting company. How ironic, how couldn't I have known? A report just got filed on him, why wouldn't he show up and wreak havoc? We checked through the peephole and through the door window. No one was there. Finally, she opened the door and as I stood hiding by the top of the stairs I heard a voice that was all too familiar. Dash, I bolted to the upstairs bathroom in fear for my life. Locked the door and sat in the tub, 7th grade was a hard year. I heard

the voices shouting back and forth at each other. Then, then I heard "matter fact, where's Alethia!?" My heart dropped. So many things ran through my mind. Demanded to exit my safe place, I pretended to flush the toilet, wash my hands then proceed- ed to leave with caution. There he was at the top of my stairs, standing in rage, living in rage, drunk in rage. It didn't end well.

The next few years I thought I wasted my time in life "figuring myself out" aka. "Falling in love with society". I thought I was on a true journey to finding me, when all I was doing was finding everyone else, and or finding someone with the criteria I thought I needed to "fill my void". It was crazy. That one very event caused me to grow into being a particular way in society. Into wanting certain things in relationships, friendships, situation-ships. I got cold, I was hard. Then I hit 9th grade and I did my own thing.

Until one day I was introduced to a group of friends. In that group of friends, a boy, when he saw me and everyone on my back...he made it known I was already his. Mind you, I didn't know him yet from a hole in the wall. I fell in love. We became high school sweet-hearts and I thought the dream would never end. Well ladies and gentlemen, it did. Year one we vibed and fell in love. Year two we made it official. How funny, as soon as we had a title things took a turn for the worse. We were 16. We couldn't see eye to eye on anything. My feelings were hurt everyday. So me, being who I was, I left. I refused to stay in something that was not making me happy. Then the next day, after I break my ties with him, there it goes he's sleeping with the enemy. So much rage. A couple weeks later I found out, boom, now I'm really the typical girl. 16 and pregnant. My whole life fell apart. Immediately out of fear and heightened emotions I scheduled an appointment for termination through planned parent-hood. They wanted $600.00. I was 16 years old with zero dollars. I scheduled the appointment regardless and him, he seemed like he wanted whatever I wanted. My sperm donor would kill me. I can't be 16 and pregnant. Getting bigger, I couldn't continue to act like this problem wasn't present and these secret appointments and prescriptions weren't taking a toll on me. I called planned parenthood and a lovely woman saved my life.

She told me there's a hospital close to me, (name disclosed), that offers free termination. My heart stopped. I'm doing this, am I really doing this? I called to schedule an appointment, but one problem. I'm a minor. I needed parental consent, or the judge's consent. Well that was an easy decision, looks like I was headed to the court. Working, 16 and pregnant was hard but I made it work. I'll never forget the phone call I made to the lawyer. I needed to get myself a lawyer to represent me before the judge. We met for Starbucks and then there we went to tackle this thing. I sat within the judge's chambers with my lawyer and the judge asked me a series of questions. My answers found that I was mature enough to make a conscious decision at 16 years old not to have a baby without my parents consent. Harmony. Now Imagine. What a soul tie. I couldn't leave him now. We were bound together through that innocent soul. He'd be my forever bind now. Forever... forever dealing with constant other females surfacing from a dead sea. Forever dealing with belligerence and rage, broken doors and hearts. Forever bickering with the only person you truly thought you had on your team? Forever fearful but dangerous all in one.

Forever in love and in lust. Forever believing the false dreams. Forever listening to "It's not the way it seems". Forever, I couldn't be that "forever" kind of girl. The morals deep within my soul could not allow it! Back and forth, I tried to walk away and go... but not from him he decided, so he followed. While walking away, he chased me. Grabbed my bag, emptied out all my belongings in public, and continued to physically push me to the ground. You see, the young me was oblivious to the literal desire for control in that very moment. The wanting to stand over my helpless body.

The want to embarrass and hurt me, physically, emotionally, and mentally all in one. Control, life was all about control. So, me being me, I searched for a way to regain my control. I searched for a new way to be that girl that fought hard for herself. I searched for the proper tools I needed to win this downhill battle. My words did not work. My strength was never sufficient. My encourage- ment was no longer existent. I gave up fighting for me, fighting for my soul's freedom. Instead, I turned more to the environment I was held hostage in. The drugs really became my encouragement as well as a source of income. The people struggling around me became my family, they felt my hurt, they understood my aban- donment element. They too themselves were alone making a way for them and the family they knew they had but felt they didn't.

Fast forward, "Alethia, can you do me a favor please!?, I need you to go clean up that throw up over there by the pool area. I am too hungover to be doing this right now". My direct supervisor, the director of operations had the audacity to speak to me, the one who fought for everything especially her respect, in that manner. You're thinking exactly what I said. It was time to go. "I am putting my two weeks notice in right now, here you go" I left the job I was working at for three years of my life high and dry. I had nothing to fall back on, no plan for income besides dipping and dabbling in the game like I've been doing. Things took a massive turn. I started taking my dipping and dabbling pretty serious. The rent was coming fast each month, electricity got higher in the summer, comcast never gave us a break on cable and let's not to mention this phone bill with four of our accounts on it. Things began cracking down on me.

Every night I spent swimming in my own tears of fear and suspense. What is to come next? Will I make the rent in enough time? Will I have to choose between lights and rent? During this time my spirit was pelted with stones. I knew not what my purpose was, I knew not what my heart needed to contin- ue each day. My old coping mechanisms failed me and life smacked me around every chance she got. So one day, I grew tired enough. I decided I wouldn't do it all on my own anymore. I decided I'd no longer break my back for people who could care less whether ogluding breathe. I wrote a couple of letters to the most significant humans in my life, my guardian, my best friend, my siblings, my ex-boyfriend, and lastly… to the streets. I set up my bathroom to be at peace. Tub water running, bubbles, candles, and let's not forget the speaker with music that constantly remind- ed me it was near the end. I kept hearing the woman sing in my ears from under the water "These are my last words to you, don't be afraid, no reason to stay things will be easier this way. I've got to run I've got to hide it will be gone all the pain inside, cause all I can see are the words you wrote to me". Those letters would be my last words to them, to everyone. Just before making my final decision, I texted my best friend how much I loved her and how much I did not want to be "here". The last time I cried to her about not wanting to be "here" I cried for hours about being in the living situation I was in and how I wanted out. I left my phone on the toilet seat and that's all she wrote. I took a deep breath and closed my eyes. I would go in peace, that's all I remembered. I would use the last few moments as a peaceful time. I needed to live my last moments in peace, the total opposite of the chaos I lived my day to day life in. Instantly the peace took over and I dozed off… water running, music playing, mind vacant, sleep. That day God sent an angel to come against the assignment of the enemy. He sent my best friend to break the devils hold. Her timing was miraculous. I woke up to banging and my best friend busting in with a towel.

She drained the tub and spoke to me softly. "I'm here A, I'm here, why'd you do this? What's going on? I opened my eyes, looked around and the water. It covered my entire body, my eye closest to the tub foundation, my mouth, and the nostril closest to the ground. I sobbed instantly. The tears were inevitable and the amount was unbelievable. Sobbing, until finally

I caught my breath. My best friend asked, "What's wrong A? Why are you crying so hard? Try and control your breathing". It took a lot, but I responded to her "You weren't supposed to save me". Instantly we both sobbed together. She covered my freezing body with a towel and encouraged me to just lay there and cry. You see, young me knew not that this interaction was one of a divine connection that God has placed in my life. I showed her the letters. We continued to sob and cry out all of the pain.

From this point Alethia began to identify and walk with God. This does not make the challenges or struggles disappear. As a matter of fact once you began to operate in your God given purpose the attacks from the enemy may intensify. When I met Alethia I can tell that the presence of God was in her life. We had a brief discus- sion and immediately she thought of a friend that I should meet because of me sharing some of my vision and the work I do in the community. She shared some her vision and her goal of writing a
children's book. At the age 21 and everything she has been through she is still standing and continuing to find her Diamonds. Alethia uses her life's experience to help individuals going through some of the same challenges. God has placed a huge vision on her heart called "City Upon Hills", remember you heard it here first.

Thank You all for contributing to The Diamond Project and giving us a piece of your life!

Made in the USA
Middletown, DE
02 May 2024